A Fairy Tale About Love

....

WEDDING GRAPHIC DESIGN

....

ARTPOWER

A Fairy Tale about Love: Wedding Graphic Design
Copyright © Artpower International Publishing Co., Ltd.

ARTPOWER

Publisher: Lu Jican
Chief Editor: Li Aihong
Executive Editor: Li Aihong, Xia Jiajia, Yang Ruizhu
Art Designer: Chen Ting, Lan Meng

Registered Address
Suites 2001, 20/F., Chinachem Tower, 36 Connaught Road Central, Hong Kong, China
Tel: 852-31840676
Fax: 852-25432396

Editorial Department
5020-5023, 5th Floor, Phase II of Art Design Center, Zhanyi Road, Luohu District,
Shenzhen, China
Tel: 86-755-25111140
Fax: 86-755-82020029

Web: www.artpower.com.cn / www.acs.cn
Sales & Distribution: overseasales@artpower.com.cn
Press & Editorial Submissions: press@artpower.com.cn / contact@artpower.com.cn

ISBN 978-988-14688-8-8

No part of this publication may be reproduced or utilised in any form by any means, electronic or mechanical, including photocopying, recording or by any information storage and retrieval system, without prior written permission of the publisher.

All images in this book have been reproduced with the knowledge and prior consent of the designers and the clients concerned, and every effort has been made to ensure that credits accurately comply with information applied. No responsibility is accepted by producer, publisher, or printer for any infringement of copyright or otherwise arising from the contents of this publication.

Printed and bound in China.

CONTENTS

Chapter One

Illustrated & Painted

001-054

·······

Chapter Two

Floral

055-118

·······

Chapter Three

Classical

119-136

·······

Chapter Four

Modern

137-202

·······

Chapter Five

Traditional with a Twist

203-224

·······

Chapter Six

Vintage Inspired

225-249

·······

PRINTING PROCESSES

Printing Processes of Wedding Graphic Design in this book are divided and indicated in following pictograms as Printing Processes are usually overlapped in their usage.

Blind Embossing	(B)	(B*)	Bookbinding
Digital	(D)	(D*)	Die Cutting
Engraving	(E)	(E*)	Embossed
Foil Stamping	(F)	(G)	Glass Engraving
Hand Drawing / Hand Finished Painted	(H)	(I)	Ink Stamping
Letterpress	(L)	(L*)	Laser Cutting
Laminating	(L^)	(O)	Offset
Papercut	(P)	(R)	Risograph
Rubber Stamp	(R*)	(S)	Screen Printing
Serigraphy Paper Craft	(S*)	(S^)	Stamping
Tied up with Twine	(T)	(W)	Waxed Paper / Wax Seal
Written with a Cutting Plotter	(W*)	(3D)	3D Printing

Shellahera Project /
Rabbit & Monday Misfit /
I+L Wedding Stationery /
Indian Wedding Invite /
Bon Voyage /
Asian Birds Wedding Invitation /
New Orleans /
Under The Stars Wedding Invitation /
Caro y Mario Wedding /
Mountain Party /
Rustic Backyard Wedding /
Jen + Levi Wedding Suite /
Aiza & Melvin Wedding Invitation Suite /
Weronika & Łukasz /
A Sweet and Fresh Wedding /
Jena & Yves /
Invitation for Wedding in Ravello /
Visual Design for Our Own Wedding /
Really Rustic Vintage Wedding Kit /
Watercolor Wreath Creator /
Hand-Painted Mauve Wedding Stationery /
Joe and Bee Wedding Invitation Suite /
Wedding Invitation for Abigail and Dimas /
Wedding Invitation for Hendra and Esa /
Wedding Invitation for Mirna and Fuad /
Wedding Invitation /

· · · · · · · · ·

Illustrated & Painted

Chapter One

Shellahera Project

Design Agency: Lostvoltype Foundry

· Simple card template I created to demonstrate the use of this font

The development of the technology makes many people want something different, as well as in the type design. Trend typography with a handmade feeling is one of the greatest needs today, especially at special moments like the wedding celebration. Many people use the services of hand letterer to write down the names for invitations, post cards, table numbers, sign panels, a photo booth backdrop up small souvenirs decorated with handmade typography.

To answer the needs that I told above, I made Shellahera Fonts. Shellahera is one of many projects that I have made the font, which features 3 different font files in a single package: Script, Sans and Ornament. This font is made by using a brush pen and scanned with high resolution to keep the detail. The combining between the art of handmade writing and sophistication of software today make the font completely different, with a feature known as Open Type Feature. This product is not only the characters to one glyph (character) but has even more than 3 different styles to each glyph. As a result, it increases the handmade feeling, because the same character in one sentence is able to have several different styles. Therefore, I'm not only to beautify this font but make it with a different baseline, which I called a dancing baseline. I also added Shellahera Handmade Sans's font in this package which can be used in conjunction with Shellahera Script as body text. Lastly, because the font was designed to meet the needs of the manufacture of typography with a handmade feeling, I added Shellahera Ornament to beautify this package.

This font had been widely used for making invitations, framed typography, and sign panels in several events, especially weddings.

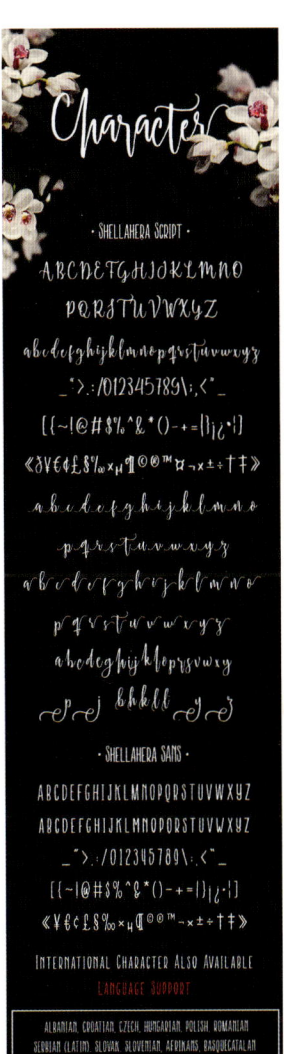

· Cover image of Shellahera Font on my portofolio & shop page

· An image to explain the character contained in this font from standard to alternate character and what languages are supported

Rabbit & Monday Misfit

Design Agency: Sciencewerk Design   Design Director: Danis Sie
Illustrator: Roby Dwi Antono   Print & Paper: Cottonville

For Danis & Tiara Wedding Event. The Rabbit mark is inspired from their Chinese zodiac. And the illustration is telling their 8-year journey. Featuring all of the couple's lovely pets: Jacob the Cockatoo, Grey the Cat, Mowgli the Dog, Guppy the Guppy, Hex Torment Anion Kation the Hamsters.

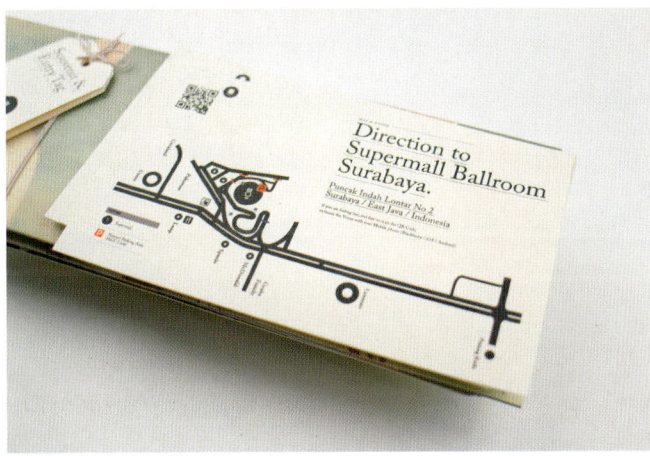

I+L Wedding Stationery

Designer: Jan Baca

I was asked by a bride-to-be to create the wedding stationery for her wedding. As she wanted it to look very unique and personal I decided to avoid the classic ways of printing and finishing. I prepared a hand-coloured paper with an uneven texture and all texts were written by a cutting plotter machine which had a gel pen mounted instead of a knife. All invitations and menu cards had a custom monogram handwritten on the other side. The result was 30 one-of-a-kind sets of announcements, menu cards and name tags.

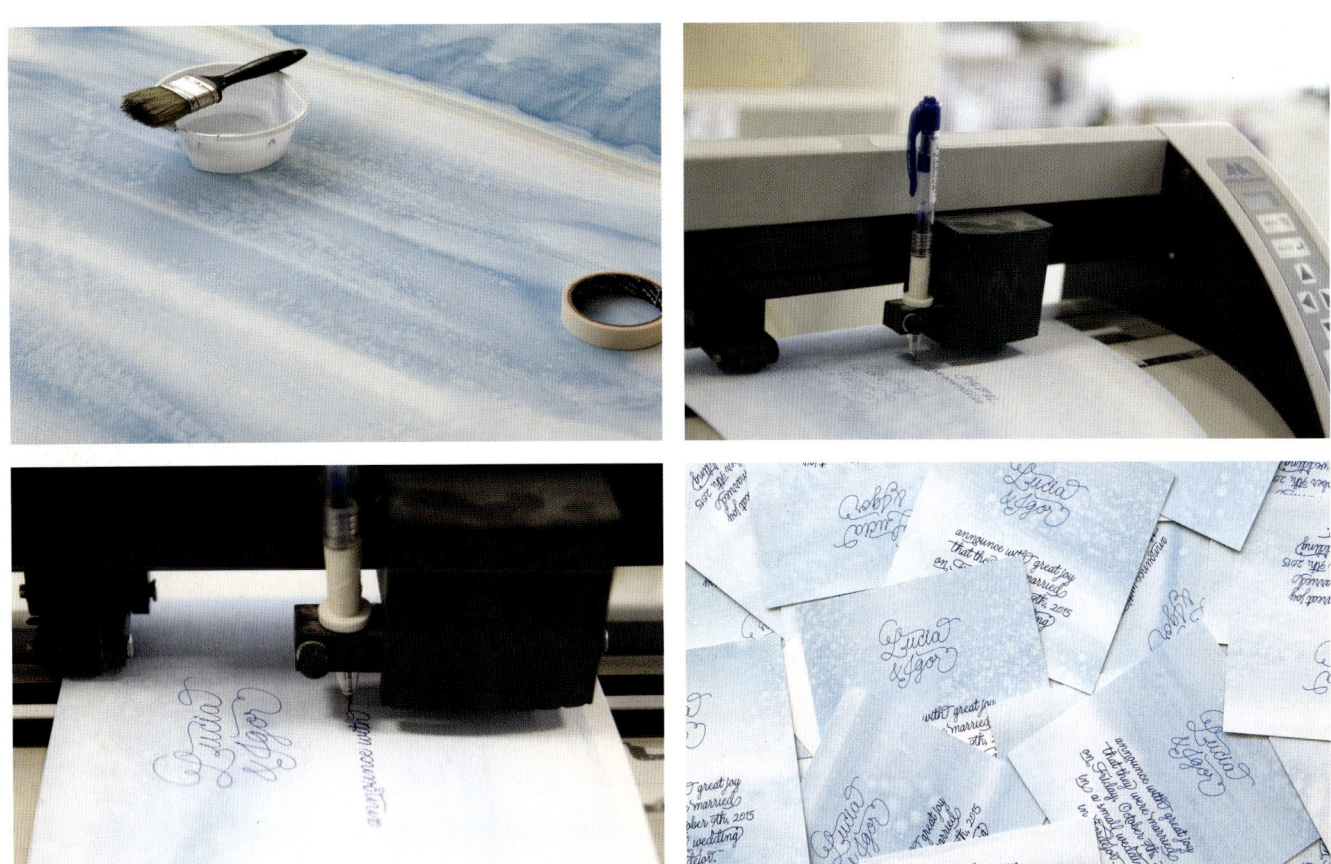

Indian Wedding Invite

Design Agency: The Kutsu   Designer: Parvati Pillai   Illustrator: Parvati Pillai
Client: Friends & Family

Sanah weds Sahil: This artwork was created as a personal project and a wedding gift for a very close friend. It included designs and illustrations for a set of collateral for a Traditional Kashmiri wedding invitation. The theme of the wedding was King & Queen of Hearts of a playing card set, so the wedding card was designed in the same size and style, and the attires of the characters in the cards had a very Kashmiri style. The design was adapted to various other collaterals of the wedding and also made way to the beautiful wishing tree on the wedding day.

Sujit weds Soumya: A wedding invite keeping the traditional South Indian culture in mind but giving it a modern-day interpretation. The bride and groom were dressed in Traditional Kerala wedding attires and we added the ribbon and floral in the design to create a modern look.

Bon Voyage

Designer: Saki Matsumoto   Client: Eri Kakuda

The couple loves the bay area chose the restaurant near the Yokohama port in Japan for the wedding party.

Then their main order for the paper items was the taste of sea, port, bay. The concept is stating the new life as the departure for a voyage.

Two seagulls which mean the bride and groom invite the visitors for the departure ceremony. Also all sea animals cheer up the atmosphere.

The cover is tied by the ribbon which is usually used for the departure celebration. The sailing ticket is used to collect the name of the attendant. Each table is separated by a sea animal and the name card has a picture with the shape of the boat.

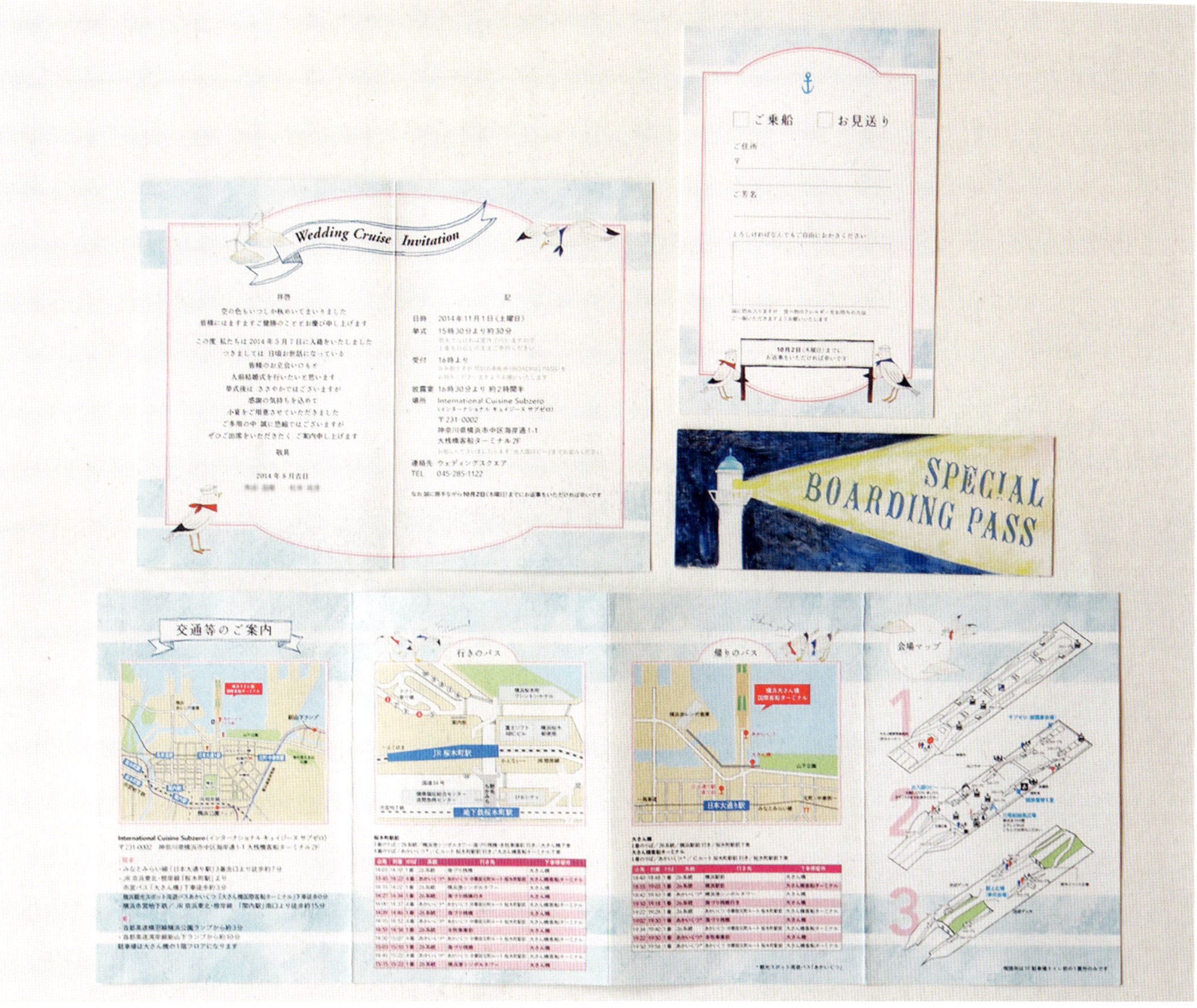

Asian Birds Wedding Invitation

Illustration: Sasha Prood Studio   Design: Southern Fried Paper
Client: Elizabeth Beaman & Julia Lake Parties

This hand-painted pattern was created in 2015 at the request of Julia Lake Parties for one of her New York-based client's wedding invitation.
The art was inspired by the wedding color palette and de Gournay bird patterns.

New Orleans

Design Agency: Atelier Isabey

Inspired by the beautiful city of New Orleans, we were tasked with creating an invitation that had both 1920s glamour and sophistication but also communicated all the important information for guests to know about the wedding. We designed a booklet drawing of the city's architecture, more notably the wrought iron façades on Bourbon Street and incorporated them in a unique and luxurious way. The suite was accented with rose gold and silver foil touches throughout.

Under The Stars Wedding Invitation

Design Agency: PaperPlate Plus   Designer: Monica Low
Illustrator: Lenny Lishchenko   Client: Monica Low

"Under The Stars" is a full wedding suite, including fold-out invitation with hand-drawn map to the venue, accommodation list, RSVP card, return envelope, and survival guide for a 3-day retreat in the wilderness. Together with the necessities, it also includes some hand-made buttons and fun star-themed tags to tie the whole design together. Sticking to the earthy palettes of navy, persimmon, aqua and cream, this wedding invitation is perfect for a quirky couple who want to make their wedding unique and memorable, before it even begins!

Caro y Mario Wedding

Designer: Matías Santiago Oddis   Client: Carolina y Mariano

2013 came with an unusual request — my sister was getting married and she wanted no one but me to work on her wedding design. So with a few few tears and a strange feeling of joy and sadness I started to work on their project. The whole thing was based on the idea of their love for France (also their honeymoon destination) and a strong concept on handmade and personal design. All cards were printed and made by hand with different finishing that went from different paper cut to watercolor painted details. Also we made personal souvenirs for the guests. A tough work that equalled the love of this event.

Mountain Party

Design Agency: HOUTH

Not like a traditional wedding, our wedding was more like an outdoor forest wedding party on the mountain. Hope everyone can dance with us in this party. We used bold color and modern illustration to design the invitation card and printed it with risograph printing.

Rustic Backyard Wedding

Designer & Illustrator: Katrin Kohl
Client: Birgit & Lukas

This wedding stationery has been created for the lovely couple Birgit & Lukas who have celebrated a traditional wedding on the countryside of Austria. Developing a logo is the first step of branding their wedding. The initials of the couple's names have been rearranged and merged in order to form a geometric heart. With the creative use of typography the logo displays how two individuals become one through love.

The invitation is placed in a transparent envelope. The first thing that catches the eyes is the small card with the logo and the date of the wedding. After unbinding the bast fiber you can fold out the invitation which reveals all the important information for the guests. The text is accompanied by quirky illustrations in the same vector-based geometric style that has already been used in the logo. That way of inviting the guests allows them to discover small details in the illustrations and get a glimpse of what they will expect on that special day.

As a give-away for the guests, the bride has prepared small jars of homemade jam, which have a tag with their logo and a "thank you" note on the backside. Like in the invitation, a bast fiber has been used to add another fabric and underline the couple's love to nature. The paper is called "Crush" by Favini, is eco-friendly and contains residues from organic materials (olives and kiwi), which match perfectly to the spirit of the rustic backyard wedding.

Jen + Levi Wedding Suite

Design Agency: Shipwright & Co.

This wedding suite was for one of our own! The entire suite was inspired by the Digby & Iona signet Jen & Levi chose as Levi's wedding ring. Each piece has alchemy-inspired designs, including the clasped hands featured on the ring which were also used in the save the date card. The couple also included elements of handfasting in their ceremony, because they felt the symbolism was especially perfect. Jen & Levi's wedding was in their backyard and very small, so they also sent out announcements to friends and family that didn't come. The beautiful flowers were provided by our friend Jaime of The Monkey Flower Group. All photos were styled and shot by Emma K. Morris.

Aiza & Melvin Wedding Invitation Suite

Designer & Calligrapher: Pauline A. Ibarra, Happy Hands Project
Client: Melvin Pereira & Aiza Domingo
Photographer: Nice Print Photography

Aiza and Melvin's wedding took place at the beautiful Boracay Island in the Philippines. The couple wanted a mix of watercolour painting and calligraphy with a carefree, beach look and feeling. The map of the island as well as the guests' attires were all hand-painted, and the suite was peppered with calligraphy to make the design more personalized.

Weronika & Łukasz

Designer: Grabovska   Client: Weronika & Łukasz Węgrzyn

Wedding invitation designed for a lovely couple Weronika & Łukasz.

Illustrations inside the invitation were personalized and inspired by Weronika and Łukasz's interests and passions. Text in the middle of the invitation was the symbolic space where they met. Illustrations which were hand drawn and painted, then digitalized and composed, became a part of the design of the invitation. Then they were digitally printed on the uncoated HQ paper.

A Sweet and Fresh Wedding

Design Agency: Pickle Films   Designer: Margarida Madeira   Client: João & Mariella

This project was born from the necessity to find an alternative to the traditional offer found nowadays in the wedding market.

The couple was looking for an original solution matching their original story. They met in Italy in the ice-cream store where João used to work to make some extra money. During the weekends, on a food truck, João sold ice-cream in the park where Mariella used to relax and walk the dog. She always asked for the same flavors: raspberry and chocolate. Eight years later, already living in Portugal, they decided to get married and nothing felt more adequate than retelling the history of their relationship.

Sketching/drawing was the basis for developing the illustrations, afterwards painted and digitally animated, according to the theme of Italian ice-cream. A short animation to be shared in social networks and sent by emails was also created as a complement to the wedding invitations.

The menu for the wedding reception was based on an ice-cream shop menu, where the customer always had the option between cup or cone as well as the number and flavor of the ice-cream scoops.

The invitation itself was the recreation of a blackboard similar to those displayed at the entrance of ice-cream shops and restaurants.

Frames from the animation created to complement the printed invitations, aimed at social media sharing and emails.

Signage was displayed in the wedding venue. It was simplistic but coherent with the theme.

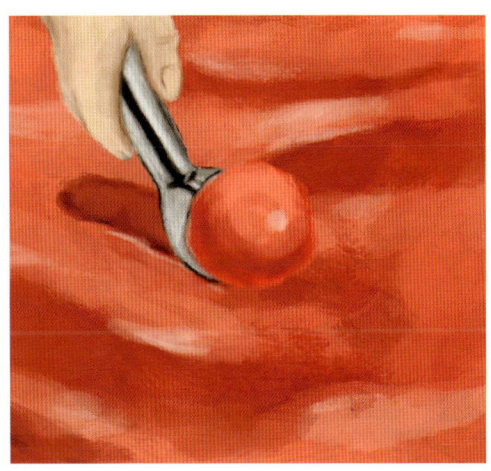

Jena & Yves

Design Agency: A Little Love Story Ltd.   Designer: Glory Lee
Photographer: Glory Lee   Client: Jena & Yves   Illustrator: Glory Lee

Oh Jena, exactly the kind of beauty that walked straight off some fancy fashion editorial, so being barely 5'2" myself… intimidated? Ah maybe a little bit, but she also brought along her laidback Californian breeze with the most generous and genuine of smiles which made our first meeting and everything onwards mega enjoyable! Jena came in with quite clear a vision of what she wanted, the brief was clear: wedding in cali (where home is) with big sur and the ocean being the perfect backdrop, floral, hydrangea, dusty pastel palette, art deco (and that has nothing to do with the great gatsby heat wave), rustic, elegant, classy, feminine. But she also allowed me to have as much creative freedom as a designer would love when it comes to creating the set. She was the precious kind that trusted me enough to adore mostly everything I built for her! Never a debate on my choice of typefaces nor graphic decisions and of course staying on schedule no matter how much travelling she's been doing! We started with some sweet bridesmaids invitations and measurement cards for prepping the perfect bridesmaid attire, then we moved on to a save the date bookmark, the main invitation set hinting at the beautiful wedding venue. And with Jena being on top of things, we were also able to echo out our set with her actual wedding flowers and decor!

Invitation for Wedding in Ravello

Designer: Sasha Boodilkina   Photographer: Sasha Boodilkina
Client: private person   Illustrator: Sasha Boodilkina

This project was made for the wedding of a couple from Spain, which was in Italy. The idea was to make a project in Italian style to underline the incredible nature of Ravello place. I chose the watercolor technique to implement the project as only the watercolor could create a sense of featheriness in the work. The goal was to recreate the atmosphere and mood of an Italian wedding. It was an attempt to make something airy, light and unusual. The bride wanted to make a themed and unique wedding where the bottles of limoncello were used as gifts to guests, and wedding tables were decorated with lemons and lemon trees grew nearby. The wedding was decorated by objects in yellow and green colors. To my mind, it was a perfect invitation to perfect wedding. The couple would like to relive their wedding. I thought this was the best compliment to the artist and organizers.

Visual Design for Our Own Wedding

Design Agency: Studio.zhenghao Creative Director: Ran & Zhi Art Director: Ran
Designer: Ran Photographer: Zhi Client: ourselves Illustrator: Ran

This design was made for our own wedding. We chose to use the hand-painted invitation, which made viewers feel close to us.

We chose to hold a western wedding in a courtyard house, and that was why we gave up using the traditional red for the major tone of the invitation. Considering the wedding was held in the summer, we decided to adopt the bright yellow as the major tone of the wedding and wedding set accompanied with the green color, white color and brown color, for yellow can bring the viewer the sense of relaxed and freshness.

Really Rustic Vintage Wedding Kit

Designer: Lisa Glanz

Some design ideas you could put together in minutes

If you're looking for an authentic, delicate vintage touch to your next wedding design, you've come to the right place! This set earns the "really rustic" title because I've been careful to retain all the lovely, authentic hand sketched details of the flowers and decorative items.

You'll receive a wide variety of items to help you whip-up a wedding stationery set in no time: from wreaths (can't have enough of those!), bouquets, 3 vintage-inspired objects, loads of hand lettered phrases and words, decorative ornaments, seamless patterns, and a set of floral numbers from 1-20 - perfect for table number place cards!

Watercolor Wreath Creator

Designer: Lisa Glanz

Create beautiful watercolor wreaths in seconds with The Watercolor Wreath Creator. It's easy to use, it's fun to use and most of all, it'll save you loads of time!

This carefully designed file is a DIY product with a difference, allowing you to create your own combos with no effort at all. Available in both Photoshop and Illustrator, only a basic knowledge of layers is required, with a full set of instructions included.

The Wreath Creator is designed either to use each layer on its own, or create more elaborate watercolor wreaths as you make each layer visible. In addition, you will receive the 60 individual watercolor elements separately, ready for you to go forth and design your heart out!

Hand-Painted Mauve Wedding Stationery

Designer: Hello it's Matilda   Photography: Dochter Photography

The bride and groom described the atmosphere of their wedding as relaxed, unconventional, with a bohemian touch. The couple wanted a hand-painted wreath that consisted of leaves and twigs that captured the colors of their wedding as well as the relaxed, bohemian atmosphere. Their colors were charcoal and mauve, with a touch of gold. The hand-painted brush lettering contributed towards the informal feel of the wedding.

Joe and Bee Wedding Invitation Suite

Illustrator: Belinda Love Lee   Art Director: Belinda Love Lee
Creative Director: Belinda Love Lee   Designer: Belinda Love Lee
Client: Joe Stratford and Belinda Love Lee   Photography: Belinda Love Lee

This wedding suite was designed for my husband & I. We wanted it to represent us without being overly floral. Thus the simplistic, minimal, illustrative qualities came most true to us. We also aimed to keep it multi-functional: the invites were designed with a rip off reminder, and the programs with a napkin to dry the eyes and confetti to celebrate! The invitations were printed on embossed 320 gsm textured cotton paper, with the inside fold printed on eco-friendly recycled texture paper. The programs were printed on a variety of 130 gsm colored paper.

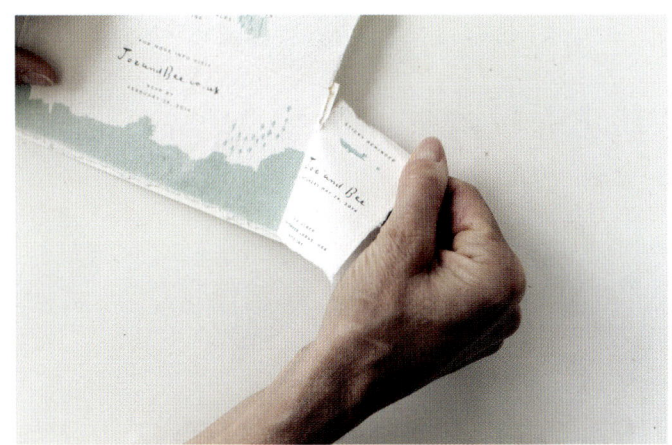

Wedding Invitation for Abigail and Dimas

Design Agency: PoLA Artistry   Creative Director: Cempaka Surakusumah
Art Director: Cempaka Surakusumah   Designer: Cempaka Surakusumah
Illustrator: Cempaka Surakusumah & Andiani Herlina   Client: Abigail & Dimas

Abigail is a radio DJ, and her hubby Dimas, is a musician. They wanted an intimate, personal, simple and still artsy party. Their decision to hold the reception at Mount Pancar was also very simple yet unique.

Their wedding theme is forest. Like the surroundings of a mountain forest, we illustrated a bear, a beaver, a pine tree, mountain flowers, and of course, ladybugs. Although you can't easily locate bears and beavers in the local forests nowadays, they hold a special place in this couple's hearts because the bear and the beaver resemble them so much.

Wedding Invitation for Hendra and Esa

Design Agency: PoLA Artistry   Creative Director: Cempaka Surakusumah
Art Director: Cempaka Surakusumah   Designer: Cempaka Surakusumah
Illustrator: Cempaka Surakusumah & Sabrina Febriyani   Client: Hendra & Esa

Hendra and Esa have the same taste when it comes down to art and music. They both love artists of the surrealist movement like Rene Magritte, Salvador Dali, and Storm Thorgerson.

Through the brainstorming process, the song "Coney Island Baby" by Lou Reed was played before us, and they asked for the song to be re-interpreted in their wedding invitation.

049

Wedding Invitation for Mirna and Fuad

Design Agency: PoLA Artistry   Creative Director: Sabrina Febriyani
Art Director: Sabrina Febriyani   Designer: Sabrina Febriyani
Illustrator: Sabrina Febriyani   Client: Mirna and Fuad

Mirna and Fuad are truly cat lovers. Not only both of them are big fans of cat, but also their families. The interesting story is that the cat actually is the important part of their relationship and love journey; even it is the reason they met for the very first time.

It started back when Mirna wanted to be introduced to the owner of a cat farm (the farm itself called Kebun Kucing – it meant cat farm in Indonesian). The owner of the farm was Fuad's mother. Fuad's mother introduced Mirna to Fuad; they met, then one thing led to another, they fell in love, and actually ended up getting married.

Therefore, we made the cat as the main theme of their wedding invitation. The invitation illustrated how two cats met at a "cat farm". Batik motif from Tasik, Indonesia inspired us for illustration style and color. The characteristics of the motif were bright, vivid, mostly nature-inspired, flora fauna themed, and modern.

Wedding Invitation

Designer: Natália Fanchini

This is one of the types of projects that I do the most.

The Illustration makes the wedding invitation something personal and unique. In this case, I use the cut mark to interact with the characters.

Anastasia & Evgeny Invitations /
Winter Wedding Invitations /
Chao & Hikki Wedding Invitation /
C + J Wedding Invites /
The KMA Wedding /
Adam & Dorian /
Federico & Noelia /
Autumn Wedding Invitation Kit /
Wedding Invitation /
Hawaiian Breeze /
Wedding Invitation /
Terrariums+Flowers Romantic Set /
Lorraine &Arthur's Wedding /
Marie & Alexandre /
Maitén & Ramiro /
Wedding Invitation for Bernardo and Isabella /
Fern Wedding Invitations /
Vine Wedding Invitations /
Gosia & Bram Wedding Invitations /
Poppie & Surya /
Wedding Stationery for Ashley & Edwin /
V&R /
Wedding Invitation and Book /
Laura & Jorge Wedding Invitation /
Amanda & Banjo /
Anita & Hendra /
Wedding Identification /
Wedding Invitation Suite "Briar" /
Wedding Invitation Suite for Wedindiy /
Wedding Invitation Suite Hellebore for Paperlust /
Floral Wedding Invitation /

....

Floral
Chapter Two

Anastasia & Evgeny Invitations

Designer: Anastasia Kolesnikova

This light and soft project was created for a nice summer wedding in bright "girls" pink colors. The rose pattern for the inner side of the envelope was made by watercolor. A huge work had been made for the logo and cover of the invitation — hand drawn calligraphy lettering. This project worked perfectly well with decor and floristics, because it was really important to save the style in each detail.

Winter Wedding Invitations

Designer: Anastasia Kolesnikova

This was a project for a stylish winter wedding, performed in cold colors by watercolor. Soft and almost transparent flowers inside the envelope were the perfect additions for the blue watercolor background in the invitation. In general, this project worked perfectly with the floristic decorations in dark colors.

Chao & Hikki Wedding Invitation

Designer: Wang Shi-Chao & Hikki Liao　Client: Own

This wedding invitation was trying to deliver the visual imagery of oriental sophistication together with modernity. The idea was inspired from the art of Chinese Seal which contained the first names of the bride and groom: Chao and Hikki. The concept of the union of two people was then brought up by combining the two strokes of letters in one Chinese Seal.

C + J Wedding Invites

Design Agency: Farhanah Designer: Farhanah Ross Client: Cynthia Russo
Photographer: Farhanah Ross

Cynthia contacted me to help design her wedding collaterals. This included the wedding invites, logo, ceremony page, menu, tags and signs which were going to be at the wedding. Cynthia had a good idea of the vibe she wanted the collaterals to have and also wanted them to match the atmosphere of Cas Xorc— the venue where the wedding would be held and where the bride, groom and attendees would be staying for that weekend. She shared examples via Pinterest of the sort of things she liked and what she felt would be fitting. This was a great help to me as it helped me envision her vision better and greatly reduced miscommunication. I felt like for this project we worked as a team, I took in the influences Cynthia had and used that to come up with a look that was tailored specifically for her wedding. The direction we went for was rustic— but not too much so— and clean. The collaterals ended up matching seamlessly with the environment and these invites gave the wedding guests a nice first glimpse into the vibe the wedding would have, before actually being present at Cas Xorc.

Together with our families, we would like to
invite you to celebrate our wedding

Cynthia & Johann

SIX THIRTY IN THE
AFTERNOON

on

SATURDAY
JUNE 25TH, 2016
CA'S XORC - SOLLER
MALLORCA

followed by

dinner + dancing + drinks

· Formal / Dunkler Anzug ·

Please join us for a

Sunset
WELCOME DINNER

FRIDAY
JUNE 24TH, 2016
SEVEN THIRTY IN
THE EVENING

at

CA'S PATRO MARCH - DEIA
MALLORCA

dress code:

summer chic / flat footwear

Transportation back to your accommodation
will be provided

rsvp

Weekend Details

FRIDAY . JUNE 24TH . 7:30PM
- SUNSET WELCOME DINNER -
CA'S PATRO MARCH
CARRER SA CALA, 16, 07179 DEIA
dress code:
summer chic / flat footwear

SATURDAY . JUNE 25TH . 12:00PM
- PAELLA BY THE POOL LUNCH -
CA'S XORC
CARRETERA DE DEIA, 56.1KM, 07100 SOLLER
dress code:
relaxed summer & swimwear

SATURDAY . JUNE 25TH . 6:30PM
- WEDDING CEREMONY -
CA'S XORC
dress code:
formal / dunkler anzug

The KMA Wedding

Design Agency: KuKi   Calligraphy and Layout: Mari Kinovych
Watercolor: Olga Kurovets   Photography: Olya Nosko

The KMA Wedding was not just a usual wedding ceremony. It was a mini-festival around a marriage of two of The National University of Kyiv-Mohyla Academy's students. It was positioned as a festival of love, tenderness and family values. The ceremony was accompanied by theatrical and musical performances, different workshops, a food court, and a dance pole. Each activity was open to everyone, not only the couple's friends and relatives.

For all the diverse activities, a unique decorative style was needed. Green, dark sky-blue and white had been chosen as the main colors of the festival.

The calligraphy and the watercolor were selected as the techniques which served well for the aim of creating a fresh, vivid and natural visual style of The KMA Wedding. Consequently, we created a combination of watercolor illustration with lettering which seemed to reflect the best of the festival's spirit (educational establishment with old history + youth + love + fun for everyone). The result gave a sensation of a craft work, and the invitations and posters seemed to have been made by hand.

During the elaboration of the project, we were struggling to find the best balance between minimalism, freshness and distinctiveness of the image, that was why we combined detailed, realistic elements with semi-transparent, largely stylized ones.

Adam & Dorian

Designer: Daniel Ioannou   Client: Adam Kuperman + Dorian Ferlauto
Photography: Daniel Ioannou

With a weekend of celebrations planned in the beautiful Californian Spring, Adam and Dorian wanted a fresh and exciting set of stationery to invite their loved ones along. Delivered in luxe cream envelopes meticulously calligraphed in black ink, the rolling greens of the Chileno Valley Ranch inspired the color palette, while the botanical illustrations alluded to the couple's vintage style decor at the venue.

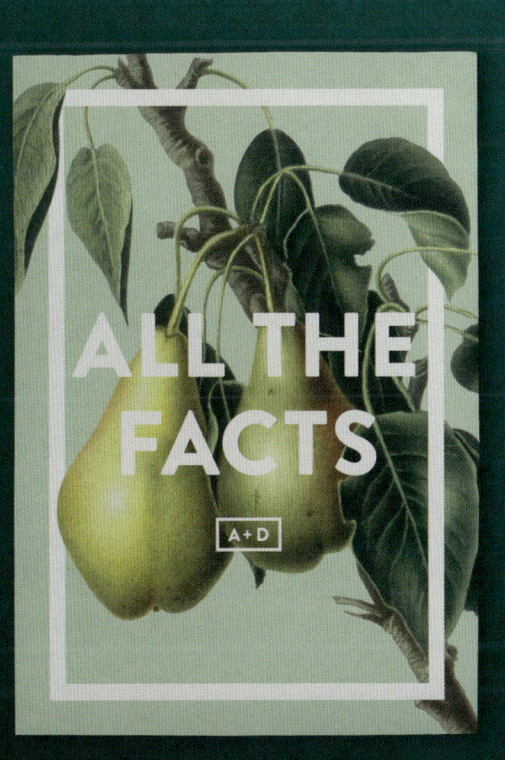

Federico & Noelia

Designer: Andrés Rossato   Client: Federico & Noelia
Illustrator: Andrés Rossato

Wedding invitation for Federico & Noelia, dear couple of friends.

Inspired by the floral ornaments from the nature, with a particular atmosphere of the colors.

Autumn Wedding Invitation Kit

Designer: Elvira Ruban   Illustrator: Elvira Ruban
Photographer: Elvira Ruban

Autumn wedding invitation kit is made for all the brides and grooms who plan to transfer a bright autumn mood and their joy through the wedding invitations.

The main motive of this project was the bright colors of autumn arctic forests. Inspiration for illustrations of this kit was found while travelling through the northern Finland and Norway in September.

This kit contained the most frequently used cards: Wedding Invitation, RSVP, Save the Date, Details, Thank you, Table number, Place Card, Menu.

The autumn leaves, delicate branches and ripe rowan berries were hand painted in watercolor with love. Then all the paintings were digitalized and put onto wedding invitation templates. There was added sample text which should be personalized for a specific customer. The fonts used for this project were Alex Brush and Cardo and can be found on https://www.fontsquirrel.com.

15

RSVP

M _____

____ Accept with pleasure!
____ Decline with regret

Please reply by 05.01.2017

Menu

STARTERS
Cornish Crab Salad
Fois Gras and Duck Confit Terrine
Spinach, Wood Mushrooms and Leek ravioli
Baked Goats Cheese

ENTREES
Pan Fried Fillet of Sea Bass
Roasted Best-End of Englh Lamb
Mignon of Devon Beef Fillet
Beef Wellington with Madeira
A Casserole of Sea Fish

DESSERT
Dark Chocolate Fond
Caramelised Crème Br
Poached Pear with licorice
Individual Passion Fruit

Details

Transportation will
to and from the we
and reception from
Also there are 40 ro
hotel.

April Winglow

SAVE THE DATE
for the wedding of
Olivia and Henry
06.10.2017
Formal invitation to follow

TOGETHER WITH THEIR FAMILIES
*Olivia Rouens
and Henry Mildale*
INVITE YOU TO CELEBRATE THEIR MARRIAGE
SATURDAY JUNE 10TH, 2017
AT TWELVE O'CLOCK IN THE AFTERNOON
THREE OAKS CLUB
12 RED MAPLE STREET
APPLESTONE
Dinner and dancing to follow

THANK YOU!

TOGETHER WITH THEIR FAMILIES
*Olivia Rouens
and Henry Mildale*
INVITE YOU TO CELEBRATE THEIR MARRIAGE
SATURDAY JUNE 10TH, 2017
AT TWELVE O'CLOCK IN THE AFTERNOON
THREE OAKS CLUB
12 RED MAPLE STREET
APPLESTONE
Dinner and dancing to follow

RSVP

M _____

____ Accept with pleasure!
____ Decline with regret

Please reply by 05.01.2017

SAVE THE DATE
for the wedding of
Olivia and Henry
06.10.2017
Formal invitation to follow

Wedding Invitation

Designer: Emília Abreu   Client: Marcela Corrente   Illustrator: Emília Abreu
Photographer: Karina Bonna

This project was created as a personal design and a wedding gift for a very close friend, the bride! I developed all the project art from the designs and illustrations to the lettering of the envelope. The bride asked me to create something with vintage flowers and modern types, a vintage and modern design with pink and blue colors. The wedding card was designed in 2 parts, the first with the invite and the second with the infos from the party. The second was smaller and with a serrated edge in the middle, so when cut in the middle it would become a bookmark and the guests would keep the bride and groom's invitation with them.

073

Hawaiian Breeze

Design Agency: In The Castle Design   Designer: Hironobu Jyounai   Client: Hiroki & Risako
Illustrator: Hironobu Jyounai   Photographer: Hironobu Jyounai

It is a wedding invitation using a waxed envelope and skeleton leaf reminiscent of Hawaiian breeze. We are super excited to show you these beautiful vintage-floral letterpress wedding invitations! We all know that greenery and flowers are important to make a wedding absolutely beautiful, and I love it when brides want to incorporate those elements into their wedding paper details!

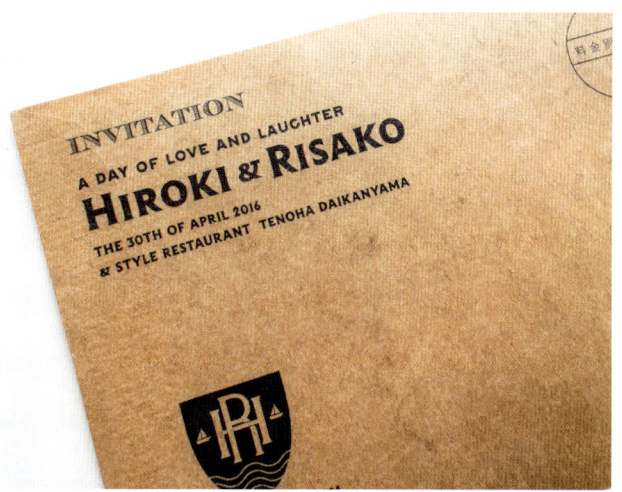

Wedding Invitation

Design & Concept: Jyoti Chandnani
Client: Roma Narsinghani

· Floral Inspiration

When I met the bride, her vision for her summer wedding was very clear: English tea party, simple, vintage and floral. The venue inspired the color scheme for the invites. The color palette included midnight blue, pistachio green, light pink and blue.

The flowers chosen by the wedding planner were bougainvillea, lavender, pansy, dahlia, silk floss and asters. So it made perfect sense to incorporate the same flowers as illustrations in the design. The wedding gown had floral details as well.

The bride requested for the tote bags and travel shoe bags for the guests. I also designed the special chocolate boxes for the event.

Terrariums+Flowers Romantic Set

Designer: Lera Efremova   Illustrator: Lera Efremova

Terrariums become very popular in recent years, so I decide to use them in nonstandard form, as a decorative element in the design of the wedding invitations. I create this graphic set as a template, so everyone can add some texts or letterings, add some items and use it as a personalized wedding invitation. I really like the combination of the strict geometric shapes and straight lines with the delicate floral elements. Together they create an interesting mood and form a harmony, and the invitations look unusual and beautiful.

Lorraine & Arthur's Wedding

Design Agency: ChokdiDesign   Designer: Thaï Ch. Hamelin
Client: Lorraine & Arthur   Photographer: Thaï Ch. Hamelin

Both Lorraine and Arthur were doctors and very passionate about fauna and flora, vintage scientific imagery of the 17th century, as well as exotic birds, which colored Lorraine's childhood in Brazil and Thailand.

Lorraine and Arthur wanted to stay close to the mood of old books from Lorraine's family castle, where the ceremony was held. The inspiration came from Haeckel's work, and more traditional chromolithographs of botanical research of the 19th century.

Everything was printed in central France and finished by hand: gift bottles containing traditional liquor were bottled on site, and mass booklets were hand sewn by the groom.

Marie & Alexandre

Design Agency: ChokdiDesign Designer: Thaï Ch. Hamelin
Client: Marie & Alexandre Photographer: Thaï Ch. Hamelin

Marie & Alexandre have a strange passion for "curiosity cabinets", old bottles and apothecaries. All the decorations are made of jars and vials with the original pharmaceutical or botanical names. We've also found old crates and dusty shelves. Marie also happens to have a passion for roses. The rose is the key element of the decoration. We've used flowers to brighten up the vintage setting of fresh in old, new in vintage.

The contrast of the rose in the old vial is a symbol of the timelessness of love. The ideal match is to use 18th century illustrations from acclaimed P. J. Redouté.

Maitén & Ramiro

Designer: Magalí Salama   Client: Marie & Alex

It's summer in Mendoza, Argentina. The weather there is so dry that cactuses grow up happily and full of flowers. Maitén and Ramiro have chosen a beautiful place to celebrate their wedding. Outside the big city, an outdoor events room is waiting for the guests. The wedding invitations reflect some of the rustic and nature spirit that the bride and the groom want to reflect along the wedding. Delivered in stamped kraft cardboard envelopes, with the inside detail of cactuses' flowers, the wedding invitation is inspired in the venue's landscape. As little cactuses are chosen as the wedding souvenirs, their bright flowers are also the inspiration for the invitation cards. The joyful flowers soften the cards. Vintage botanical illustrations are taken from vintageprintable.swivelchairmedia.com and made the collage composition. Classic san serif font is chosen and it is blended with a calligraphic one to make an elegant and simple design. The paper chosen is a 300 grs fine texture cream cardboard. There is a small card with the number of the guests inside each envelope which is made of the same material as the envelope and it is also stamped with the same motive as well. Table number signs are designed too. All pieces are laser printed. The wedding invitation card is a nonprofit project, the designer is the couple's friend and this is her wedding's present.

Wedding Invitation for Bernardo and Isabella

Design Agency: Isabella Teles | Graphic Design   Designer: Isabella Teles
Client: Bernardo Cândido and Isabella Teles   Illustrator: Isabella Teles
Photographer: Isabella Teles

The wedding invitation, for Bernardo and Isabella, was developed in April 2015. The concept of the design was delicacy, flowers, garden, nature, treasure and harmony. I created the logo, the save the date card, the invitation, the menu, tags for presents, notebook messages wedding, labels for olive oil and website. Inside the invitation box was a photo with a vintage frame. Below the frame was a small leaflet with precious tips. Under the leaflet was an invitation card with some poems. On the other side was a poster with another poem with fine illustrations.

Fern Wedding Invitations

Design Agency: Hello Tenfold   Creative Director: Ellie Snow
Art Director: Ellie Snow   Designer: Ellie Snow
Photography: Lissa Gotwals

The Fern wedding invitations by Hello Tenfold began with the simple, black and white sketches of ferns, which designer Ellie Snow then used to create this modern wedding invitation suite. To add texture and interest, a translucent vellum wrap held all of the cards together inside the envelope, and was wrapped with thin metallic gold threads and sealed with a gold wax seal. This wedding invitation set managed to feel both traditional and modern, with a unique blue and pale lavender color scheme.

Vine Wedding Invitations

Design Agency: Hello Tenfold   Creative Director: Ellie Snow
Art Director: Ellie Snow   Designer: Ellie Snow
Photography: Lissa Gotwals

The Vine wedding invitations by Hello Tenfold featured intertwining illustrations of vines, printed in bold blues and yellows, with metallic gold foil running through the vines. A paper band held the cards together inside the envelope. This wedding invitation set combined a traditional, botanical motif with modern, sans serif fonts. The silhouetted illustrations kept the botanicals fresh, while the gold foil added a pop of interest.

Gosia & Bram Wedding Invitations

Graphic Design + Art Direction: Nina Gregier   Photography: Piotr Kierat

Gosia and Bram are a Polish-Belgian couple. They married in Belgium and later had the traditional Polish wedding party in Poland. Graphic design of the invitations referred to the atmosphere and interior design of the room where the wedding party took place. The room was full of wild flowers, colorful decorations in a rustic, yet traditional style. All materials were printed on a creamy-pink paper and orange envelope was a strong, funny accent. Small pebbles on the pictures related to the place of the bride and groom's residence – the Belgian seaside.

Poppie & Surya

Design Agency: Hari Bahagia

The couple wanted a whimsical and elegant wedding with the beauty of tropical nature. Following the theme of the wedding event, this wedding invitation was created with a pleasant touch of tropical vintage style. The flower represented the name of the bride and groom Poppie and Surya (in Indonesian means sun). Using botanical illustration style, this invitation captured the vintage vibe but still had a modern shape.

"and we created you in pairs"

Wedding Stationery for Ashley & Edwin

Design Agency: Aurora Creative Studio   Designer: Lize-Marie Dreyer

This wedding stationery features South African kingfishers as well as plants indigenous to the Bushveld, South Africa.

V&R

Designer: María Hernández   Illustrator: María Hernández
Client: Virginia & Ramón

This is a wedding invitation design for a couple who met and had their first conversation under an olive tree.

The design reflects the beautiful story of how they met, through a simple and emotive language, and the olive leaves tell us about the history of Virginia and Ramón. The illustration reflects a classic yet contemporary style thanks to the saturated and unreal colors of the leaves.

The initials of the bride and groom (VR) form a unique symbol that communicates the union of the couple.

Wedding Invitation and Book

Designer: Anna Shuvalova

The invitation and the guestbook were created for the wedding that took place in St. Petersburg, Russia, in the late autumn. The gridelin, brown and snow-blue colors made one feel the spirit and the mood of this time of the year with poetically dismal weather, dull sky and naked trees all around. The pencil illustrations were created specially for the project. Combined with A (the first letters of the couple's names), they became the key pillars of the event's identity.

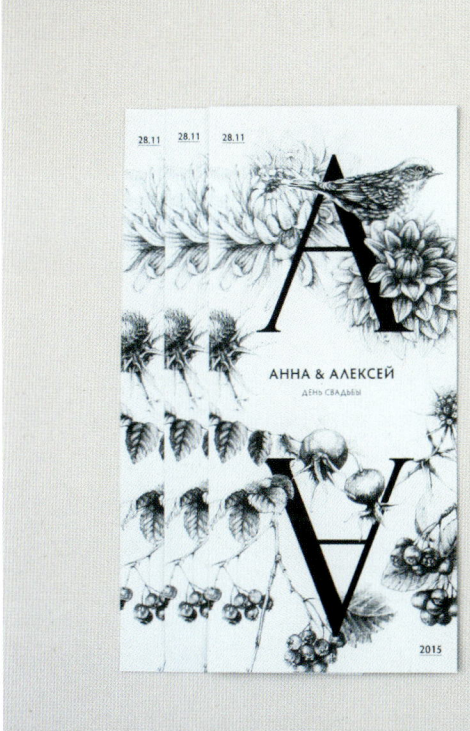

Laura & Jorge Wedding Invitation

Design Agency: INFAME STUDIO   Creative Director: Nidia Donado
Art Director: Santiago Amaya   Illustrator: Santiago Amaya
Client: Jorge Salcedo & Laura Montoya

Laura & Jorge's wedding invitation has the symbols of their love story: the coffee stain talks about when they met in a coffee shop in Bogotá; the clock represents the passing of time and the winter solstice when they got together; the feather pen indicates when Jorge went away to study and sadly they had to be separated; the compass represents the trips made together and the flowers symbolize their love for each other.

Amanda & Banjo

Design Agency: PoLA Artistry   Creative Director: Cempaka Surakusumah
Art Director: Cempaka Surakusumah   Designer: Cempaka Surakusumah
Illustrator: Cempaka Surakusumah   Client: Amanda & Banjo

Yearning for a wedding in the open garden, Amanda & Banjo wanted a theme for their wedding reception which was something that related to the spring. So, they chose "spring field" as their wedding theme and the vivid colors of the flowers illustrated in the invitations were inspired by the woven silk sarongs of the Bugis Makkassar tribe.

Anita & Hendra

Design Agency: PoLA Artistry   Creative Director: Sabrina Febriyani
Art Director: Sabrina Febriyani   Designer: Sabrina Febriyani
Illustrator: Sabrina Febriyani & Andiani Herlina   Client: Anita & Hendra

Anita and Hendra wanted a rustic garden theme for their wedding. They picked rose and hydrangea (both represent love, faith, beauty and timelessness). They also chose silver dust plant to be embedded into the design because that plant represents happiness.

Inspired by the vines, leaves and various flowers of a botanical garden, we also used green, peach and gold colors and added the rustic touch by using recycled paper.

Wedding Identification

Designer: Aleksandra Lampart-Blaźniak & Artur Blaźniak

What happens when two designers get married? It creates a modern, beautiful identification, with the nice details. The wedding identification is based on the floral rosette. The result includes the following materials: invitation, mini vodka, packaging for cakes, album, guestbook, vignette, table number, menu, poster and plate, gifts for the guests.

Each table has its theme - a particular flower. The menu consists of the names of the guests and the table numbers. However, the main motive is the wedding rosette - a collage combining all the flowers.

Wedding Invitation Suite "Briar"

Designer: Kateryna Savchenko

Here in Norway briar is everywhere and it blooms so beautifully in August and one of those grows right next to my front door. There was no actual client for this wedding invitation, just my inspiration that I couldn't stand. The illustrations were made with watercolors and calligraphic pen and I got so excited that developed a whole suite in three color modes: brown (which was original), blue and cream.

Wedding Invitation Suite for Wedindiy

Designer: Kateryna Savchenko

It's a start-up project. We have a great team and for now we work without salaries. I believe that the most important is to have freedom for your creativity and that's why I love this project.

113

Wedding Invitation Suite Hellebore for Paperlust

Designer: Kateryna Savchenko

This set features a soft turquoise floral design. I want to step away from my favourite pink and choose the hellebore as a main flower of the wreath. I believe this set is perfect for any outdoor or countryside wedding. The uses of the soft pallet, watercolor and calligraphic text make this invitation effortlessly romantic.

Floral Wedding Invitation

Designer: Raxenne Maniquiz   Client: Paulo Santos

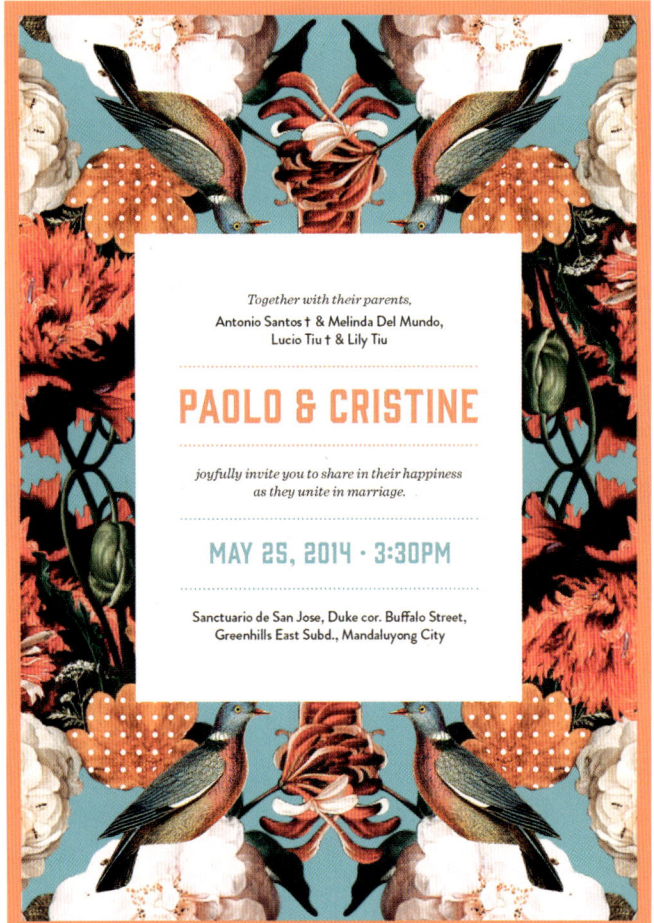

This was one of the two studies for a wedding invitation commissioned by a former client. I wanted to create a romantic collage consisting of the vintage cutouts, anchored by a clean, simple layout.

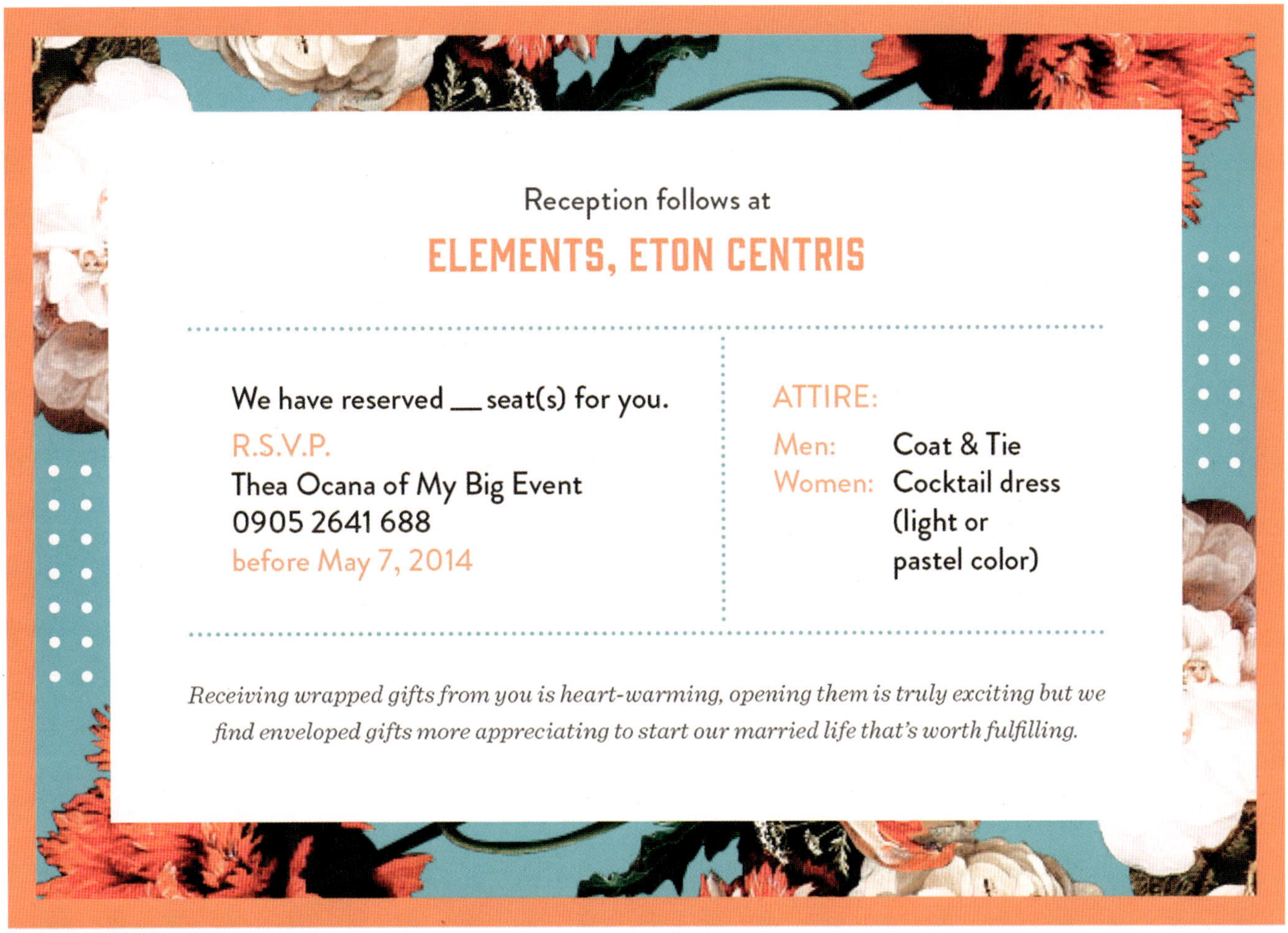

Reception follows at

ELEMENTS, ETON CENTRIS

We have reserved __ seat(s) for you.

R.S.V.P.
Thea Ocana of My Big Event
0905 2641 688
before May 7, 2014

ATTIRE:
Men: Coat & Tie
Women: Cocktail dress (light or pastel color)

Receiving wrapped gifts from you is heart-warming, opening them is truly exciting but we find enveloped gifts more appreciating to start our married life that's worth fulfilling.

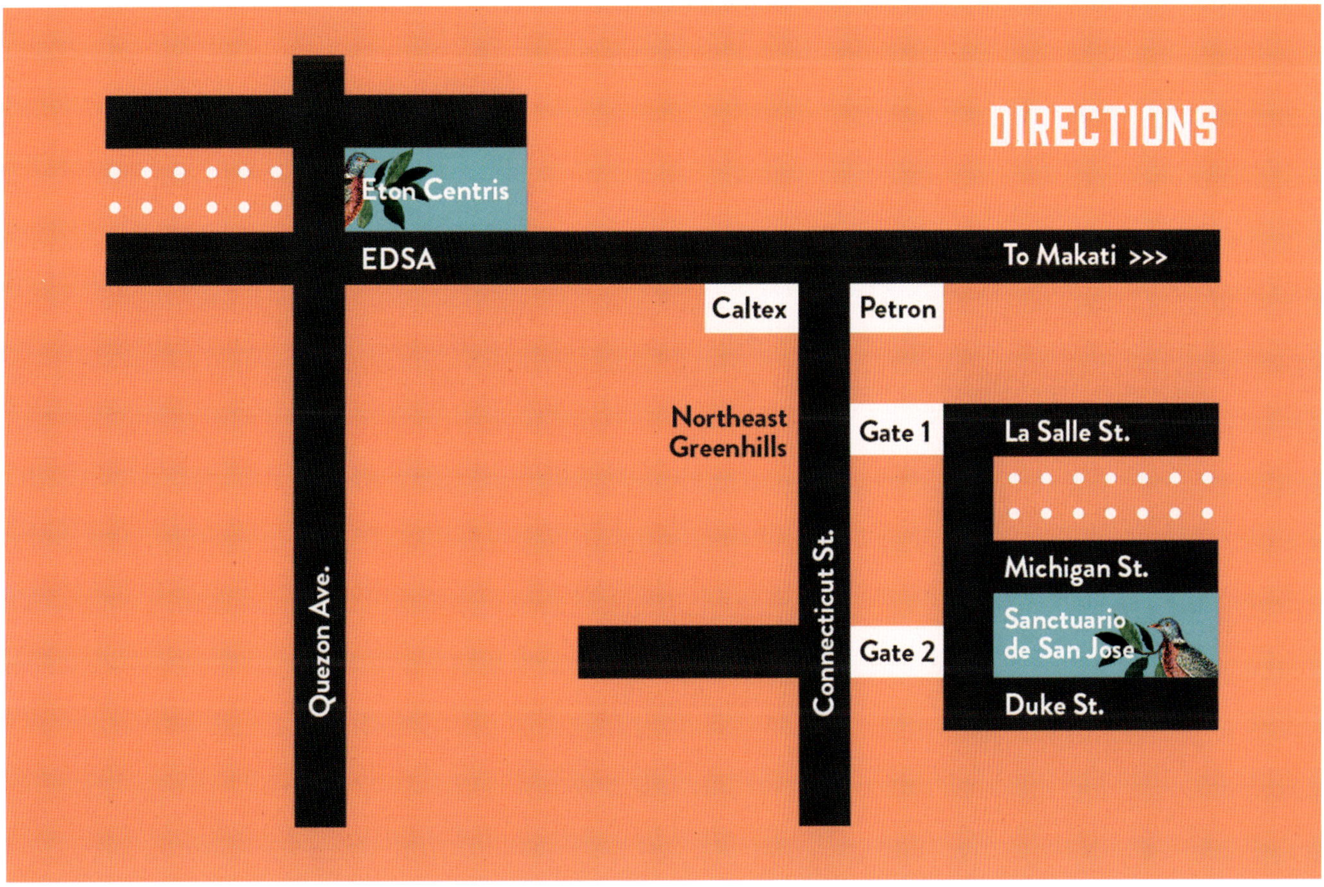

DIRECTIONS

Eton Centris
EDSA
To Makati >>>
Caltex
Petron
Northeast Greenhills
Gate 1
La Salle St.
Michigan St.
Gate 2
Sanctuario de San Jose
Duke St.
Quezon Ave.
Connecticut St.

Qing Dynasty /
Cristina & Oscar Wedding Invitation/
Niko & Monica Wedding Invitation /
Wedding Pass for Vic & Eva /
Folder Wedding Invitation for Engrácia & Valerio /
Julia & Sebastian Wedding Stationery /
Wedding Invitation Design and Rustic Decoration Design /
Dian & Wicak

....

Classical
Chapter Three

Qing Dynasty

Design Agency: Atelier Isabey

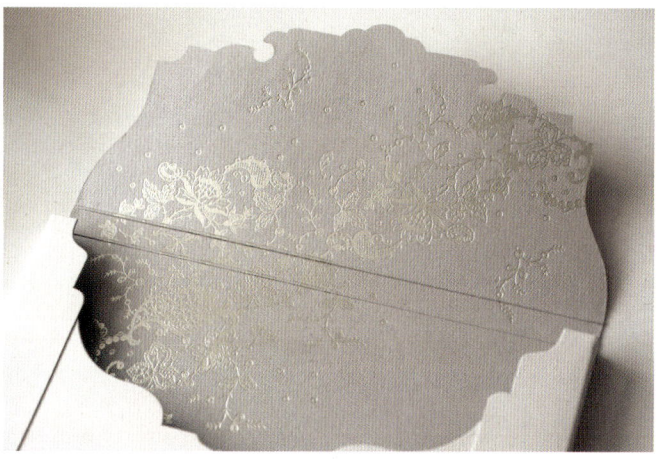

We were excited when this couple came to us looking to create a wedding invitation that captured a feeling of elegant romance while also incorporating Chinese culture and heritage. We illustrated their location by hand. It is a gorgeous estate in England, but in a traditional Qing Dynasty style. Throughout the invitations, we incorporated reinterpretations of Chinese historical motifs (from the laser cut latticework pockets, to an elegant qipao closure on the cover) in letterpress and a one-of-a-kind, custom mother-of-pearl foil.

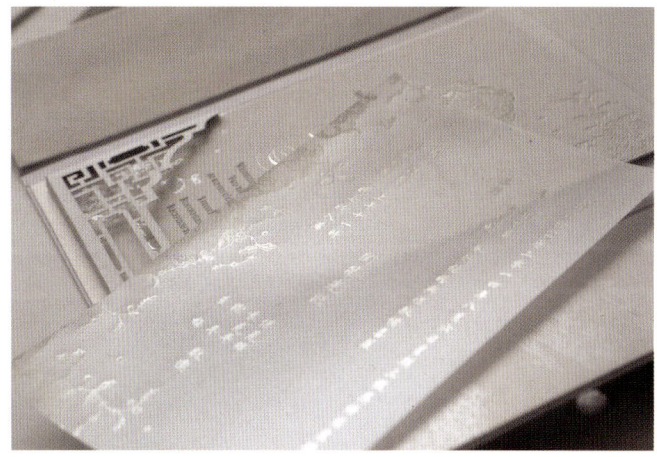

Cristina & Oscar Wedding Invitation

Design Agency: Creanet

Cristina and Oscar contacted us in late 2013 and told us that they wanted us to design their wedding invitation. And, at the first meeting, they said that their marriage would be conventional: a traditional and elegant ceremony.

We worked on different ideas that represented that concept and finally we selected the one we showed below: the ornamental letters with a classic style. We opted for this proposal because, in addition that it conveyed the concept that we thought it had to transmit, both elements fit perfectly. So, we took the sketches we had as a starting point to draw the letters, with the names of the couple and discreetly we included the necessary information for the day (date, time, location and contact information) on the bottom.

The invitation consisted of a trifold and was tied with a golden ribbon. On the back was the logo of initial C and O, and inside all the information regarding the wedding appeared.

Niko & Monica Wedding Invitation

Design Agency: KYUB Studio   Designer: KYUB Studio
Client: Niko Matias & Monica Sulaeman   Photographer: KYUB Studio

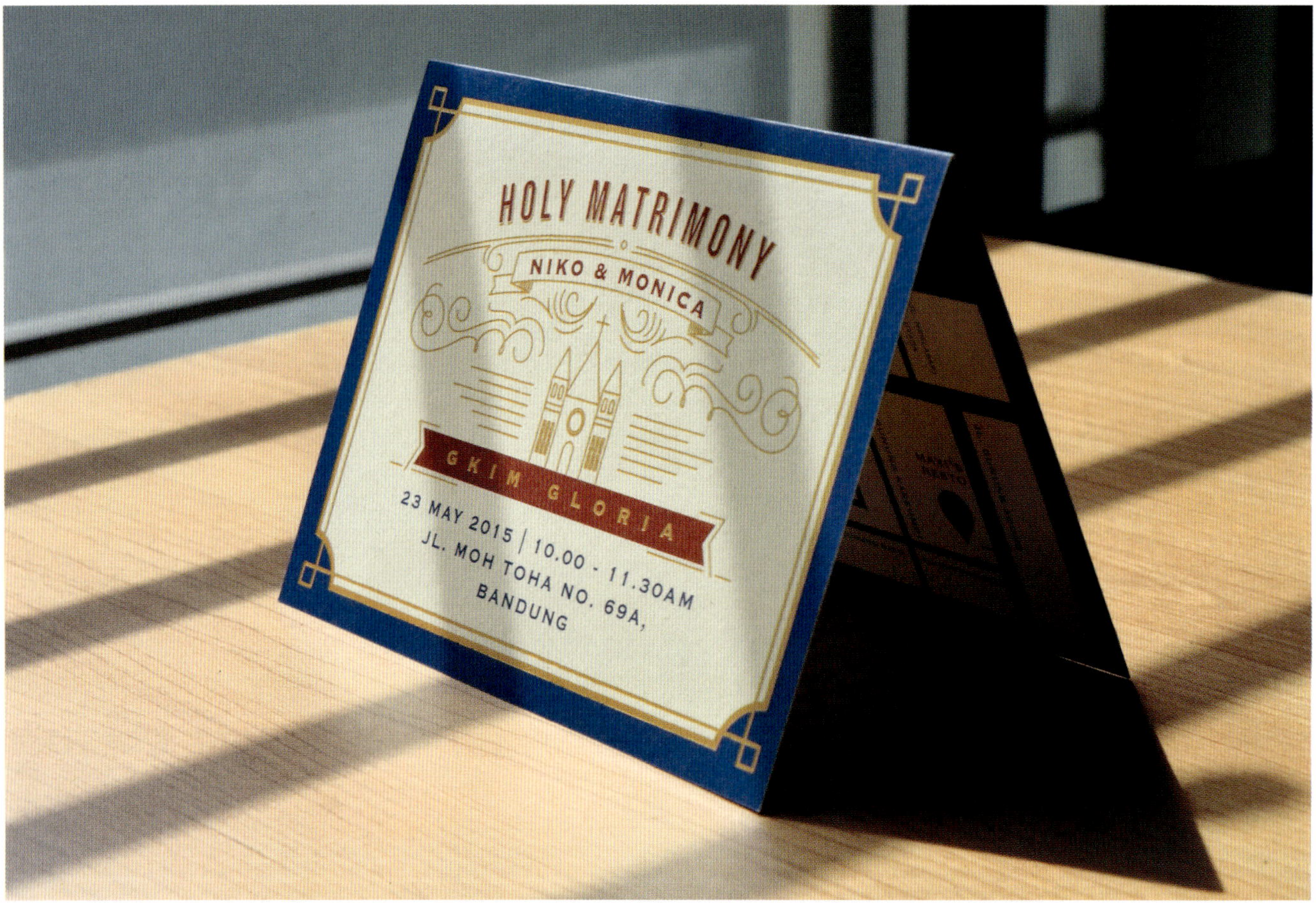

The client requested that the design contained: Paper plane, which was their love symbol; Red & Blue, their favorite color; Some degree of complexity and patterns to represent merriness and happiness. We used curly lines to represent the flow of the planes which were also used to embellish the whole look of the invitation. The consistency of the line thickness was used to maintain the modern look while also to fill up the space to achieve a certain degree of complexity.

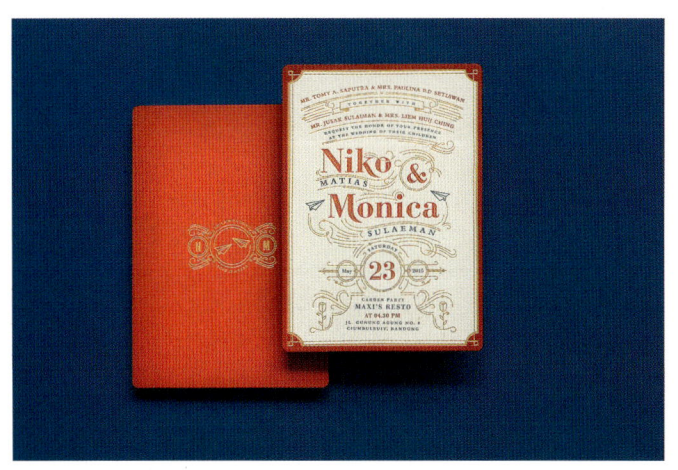
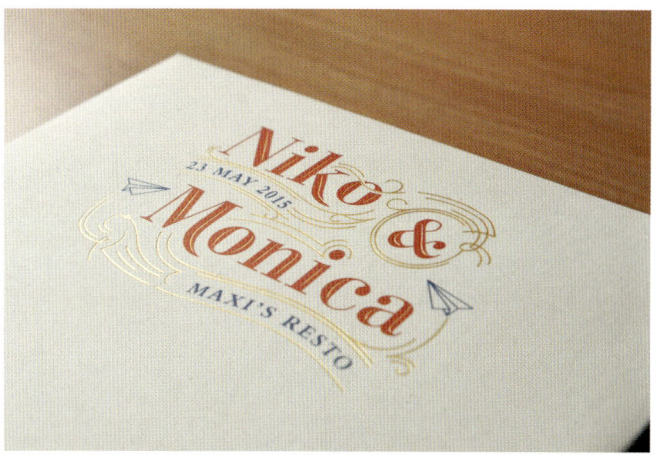

Wedding Pass for Vic & Eva

Designer: Yi-Hsuan Li   Client: Vic Tsai / Eva Chen   Photographer: Shengyuan Hsu

Wedding Pass was a wedding invitation card designed for Vic and Eva. With the high-quality, beautiful texture and complicated printing processes, the card showed our sincerity and gave them an impressive experience. Furthermore, for different ages of the invitees, we designed four different sets. The main card was designed as a ticket, and the small card was designed as a bookmark. We hope these cards can be an art collection after the wedding.

Folder Wedding Invitation for Engrácia & Valerio

Design Agency: etc & co   Designer: Filipa Sobral & Maria Moura
Client: Engrácia & Valerio

Engrácia and Valerio's invitation was meant to be classic and have a somehow regal feel. We were asked to use white and silver as the main colors as there should only be a touch of color in the satin ribbon on the outside. As we discussed some ideas with the couple, it became clear that the invitation had to make an impression. It had to be sumptuous and elegant as well as sophisticated and mature.

As the couple wanted to include a small booklet with some information about them and the wedding, we decided to design a folder with an inside pocket. This allowed us to use a bookbinding fabric in silver that had a slight shimmer and an abstract pattern for the outside. Adding a satin ribbon and a rhinestone slider to close the invitation, the cover suddenly had the elaborate look we were going for.

Inside, the main invitation had a blind embossed graphic pattern as the floral elements were out of the question. This pattern allowed us to

keep the design a bit more timeless as it blended nicely with the silver foil text.

The typography was classic and combined serif with cursive letters, which was used for the monogram. The couple's initials were used in silver foil on the cover, and they were blind embossed in the main invitation and were offset printed in the booklet being presented throughout the invitation suite.

The booklet was printed in one color only – a metallic charcoal Pantone – and was stitched in a grey silver thread.

The result was an invitation with multiple elements that came together by the use of color and design. It was the kind of invitation that could not go unnoticed.

Julia & Sebastian
Wedding Stationery

Design Agency: Skyscraper J Design Designer: Sebastian Jakl Client: Private
Illustrator: Sebastian Jakl Photographer: Sebastian Jakl

Julia & Sebastian liked it solemn and graceful. The dignified ecclesiastical ceremony was followed by an extended life affirming and jolly celebration. This was not only reflected in the intimate embracing of their merging first names' initials in their bespoke logo, but also in the way this premium wedding stationery was produced. A gold foil and full tone engraving established the detailed logo and their individual eternal motto, a poem by William Shakespeare, was printed on the high quality paper with an original 1950's Heidelberg.

Wedding Invitation Design and Rustic Decoration Design

Designer: Katja Dekhtiarenko   Photography: merveandnils.com

The design inspiration came from the cozy forest, pungent smell of the leaves and intimacy of the moment filling the atmosphere with the special romance.

Dian & Wicak

Design Agency: Hari Bahagia

In Indonesia, wedding is not just "tied a knot" between two persons. It is a family matter that involves people in many aspects. So, in relation to that, this invitation was created with a mixture of old and new elements, preserving a long lasting tradition yet bringing out a simple and beautiful expression in people's most important ceremonial in their life. The invitation was designed with unique popup decorations to accommodate the information about the wedding plus the photos of the couple. Finishing with the application of gold and silver elements into the design, the invitation showed the reflection of luxury with intense personality to the overall concept.

Kai+Tuan Wedding Invitation /
Carnation Wedding Stationery /
Typographic Wedding Stationery /
Aitor & Nerea /
Jonpaul & Anica /
Annabelle Collection Letterpress and Watercolor Wedding Suite /
Eva Collection Letterpress Wedding Suite /
Rebecca Collection Letterpress Wedding Suite /
D & U Wedding Stationery /
Wedding Invitation Set /
François & Kelly /
Maritime Wedding Series /
Luxury Wedding Invitation for Cat-lover /
Erickson Wedding Invitation /
M+M Invitations /
Wedding Invitation for Juan y Alicia /
Wedding Invitation for M & J /
FUN /
Júlia & Ricardo /
Susana & Pedro /
AC /
The Year in Love & Thanks /
Wedding Anniversary Papercut /
Papercut Wedding Artwork /
London Themed Papercut Wedding Invitation /
Food Inspired Papercut Wedding Invitation /
Papercut Wedding Invitation /
Luggage Tag Save the Date /
Brantley /
Folder Wedding Invitation for Jandira & Pitter /
R & R Wedding Invite /
Kirstin & Pablo /

··········

Modern

Chapter Four

Kai+Tuan Wedding Invitation

Design Agency: Studio moho   Designer: Ray Yen   Client: Wei-Kai Huang, Tuan Shiang
Photographer: Su-Lan Yu

The Chinese character " 囍 " is a wedding mark that represents the double joyfulness/ happiness. The couple is Christian, therefore we combined a cross symbol into the character, implying that the God will protect them and bless their marriage.

As for the format of the wedding invitation, the couple met each other since their student time, therefore we decided to represent the pure love between them. The idea was based on the folding lover letters which were used to pass notes by school boys and girls.

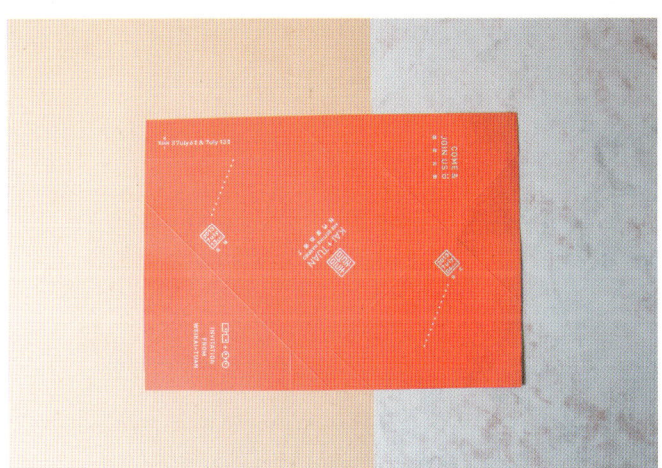
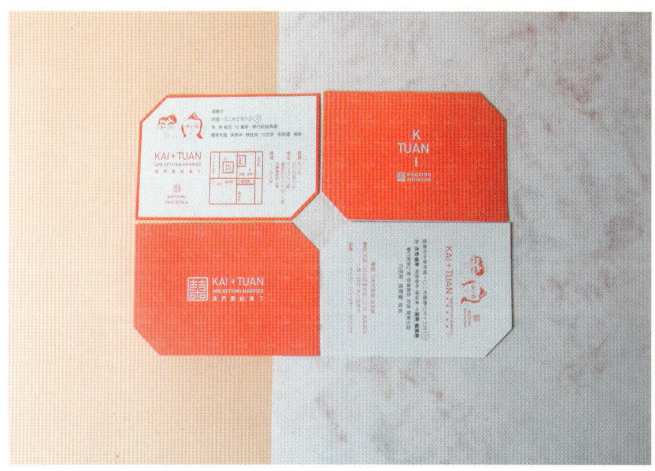

Carnation Wedding Stationery

Design Agency: SA Design Studio   Designer: Spyros Athanassopoulos
Client: Mess Project

This is a black and white modern invitation with the carnation photography on, and a fresh approach for Emma and Aaron, a young couple based in the United States.

The brief was to design a wedding set clean, modern with a dreamy touch plus a minimal initial logo for several applications. I came up with this black and white nature design in order to keep it elegant. Strong typographic elements completed the whole design.

EA
31/1/15

ron
lace

wedding

January 31st 2015 At 3.30 in the afternoon
Waverley estate 58 water port rd, Pt Eliot 5212
—
Dinner, drinks & dancing to follow, until midnight.

RSVP

M..

We wouldn't miss it for the world ☐
We will be toasting from afar ☐

Any special Food requirements' or allergies
please specify so we can best cater for you
....

Meeting point you wish to be picked up from:

The Anchorage ☐
Hotel Elliot ☐
Middleton tavern ☐
Goolwa central motel ☐

**Please RSVP
By December 15th 2014**

We look forward to celebrating with you!

Along with their parents

**Emma
Gannon** AND **Aaron
Wallace**

Invite you to join them as they celebrate their wedding
—
January 31st 2015 At 3.30 in the afternoon
Waverley estate 58 water port rd, Pt Eliot 5212
—
Dinner, drinks & dancing to follow, until midnight.

Typographic Wedding Stationery

Design Agency: SA Design Studio   Designer: Spyros Athanassopoulos
Client: Mess Project

You may say that this project is a super modern approach when it comes to the wedding stationery but the main goal is to deliver a unique and different look for young couples who want to have rather a party than the typical wedding ceremony.

It is a white and minimal design with the broken typography on. Looks like you are going to a modern music event with the main information bold which makes it easy to read despite the beautiful mess.

JASON&VICKY

Aitor & Nerea

Design Agency: La caja de tipos   Creative Director: Ander Sánchez and María Sácz
Art Director: Ander Sánchez and María Sáez
Designer: Ander Sánchez and María Sáez
Client: Aitor Sasiain and Nerea Bereziartua   Photography: María Sáez

Aitor and Nerea contacted us in late 2014 and told us that they wanted us to design their wedding invitation. And, at the first meeting, they said that their marriage would be unconventional: a casual and elegant party. Something like a cocktail.

We worked on different ideas that represented that concept and finally we selected the one we showed below: a Martini glass with a slice of lemon (to represent the cocktail) and a heart (to symbolize the union). We opted for this proposal because, in addition that it conveyed the concept that we thought it had to transmit, both elements fit perfectly. So, we took the sketches we had as a starting point to draw the illustration, we wrote below the names of the couple and discreetly we included the necessary information for the day (date, time, location and contact information) on the back.

When we had to choose the paper for the invitation we selected a 300 grams and white Conqueror Connoisseur for the front and a 240 grams Pop September Poppy (red) for the back. And for the printing, except for the heart that was embossed, we opted for the letterpress.

Jonpaul & Anica

Designer: Danny Jones   Map Illustration: Kenesha Sneed

These are wedding invites and save the dates for LA-based Photographer + Producer couple Jonpaul and Anica. Oh and their pug: Stella!

The inspiration came from Palm Springs color hues and I blended that with some handmade marbling.

Annabelle Collection Letterpress and Watercolor Wedding Suite

Design Agency: Miks Letterpress + Designer: Mariko Iwata
Stationery photos: Rachel Lynn Photography
Floral: Taffy Floral
Calligraphy: Meant to be Calligraphy

The inspiration for this wedding suite was drawn from the couple themselves. The bride wanted a soft watercolor look, while the groom wanted something more modern. I married the two concepts (pun intended) and came up with this wedding suite. It included the soft flowy feature the bride wanted with the watercolor and the crisp design element the groom liked with the white space where the text was.

The watercolor was printed digitally on cotton paper and the text was letterpressed to give a 3D texture to the suite with the impression. The neutral grey tone vintage stamps were incorporated to compliment the pink color scheme and did not take attention away from the main feature—the pink watercolor. The calligraphy on the envelopes could have gone both ways, either a soft flourishing style or a modern style and we went with a softer look.

I had a great time working on the photo shoot to put this together. It was truly a collaborative process with Taffy Floral styling the shoot incorporating not only flowers and foliage, but also various color spices. Rachel Lynn Photography made sure that we had the right lighting and the calligraphy really hit the spot with Meant to be Calligraphy.

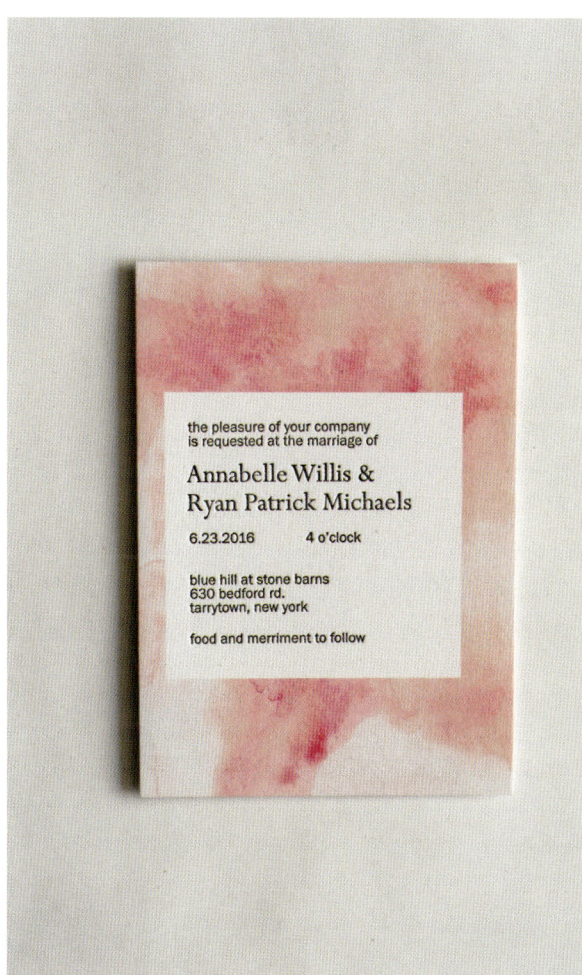
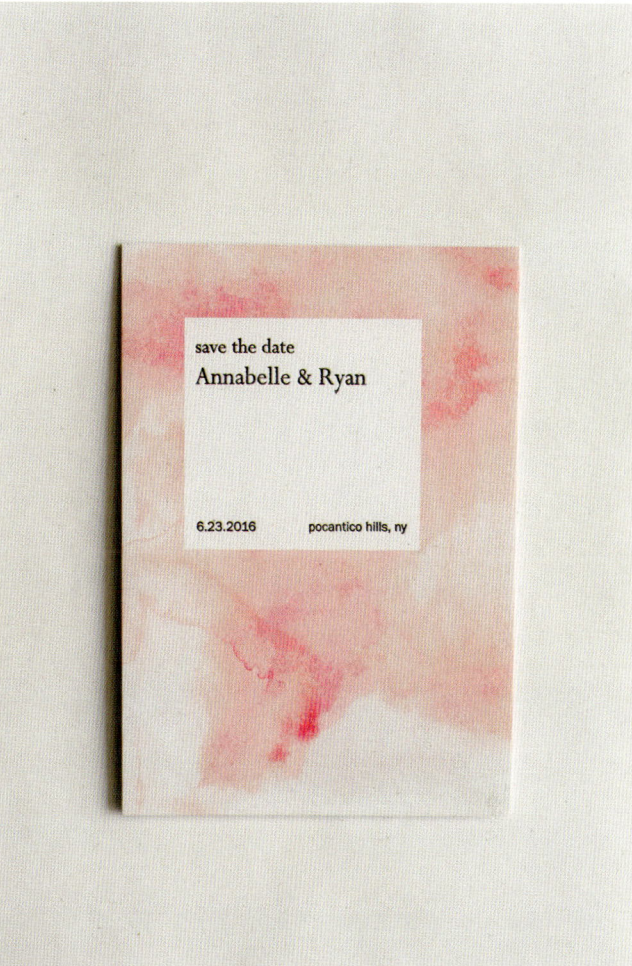
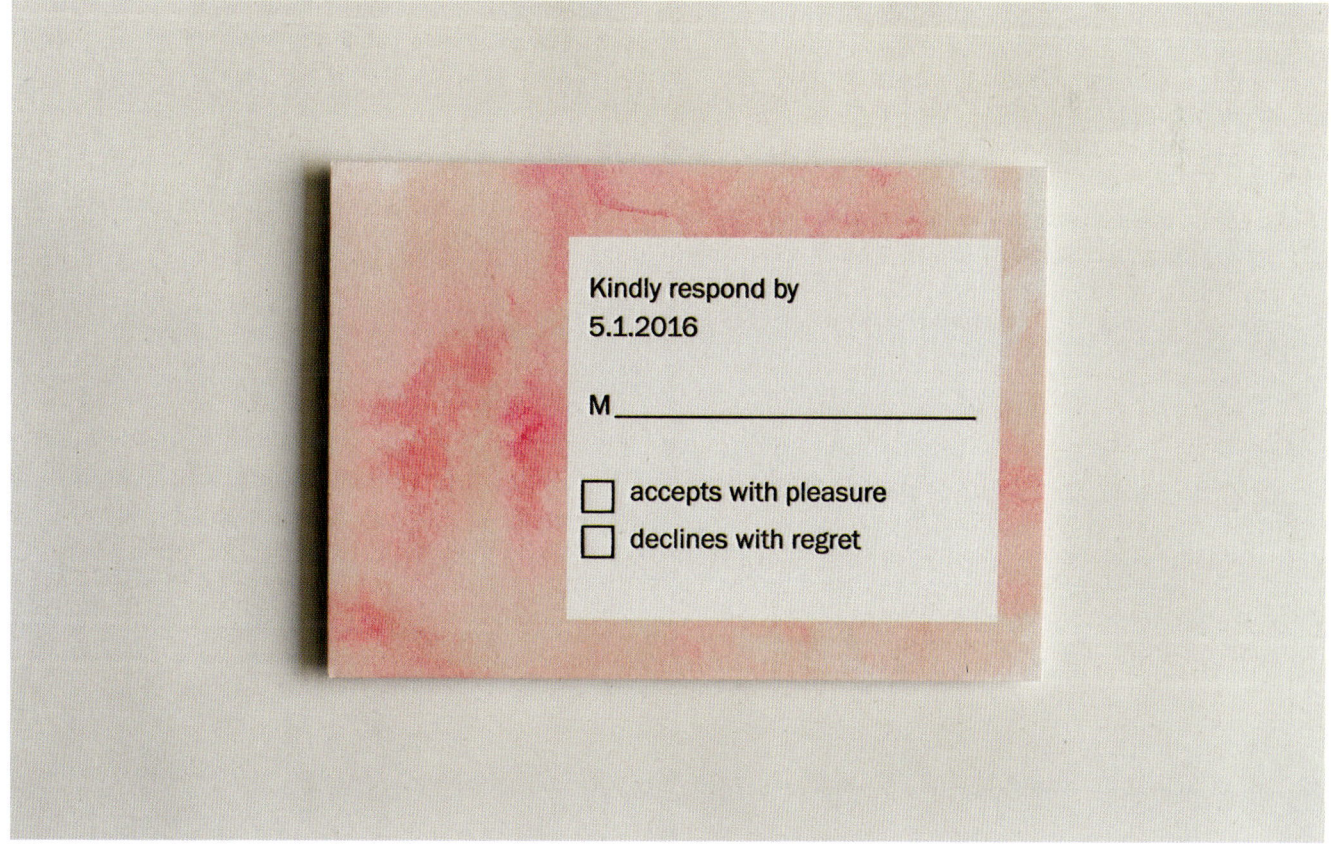

Eva Collection Letterpress Wedding Suite

Design Agency: Miks Letterpress + Designer: Mariko Iwata
Stationery photos: Rachel Lynn Photography
Floral: Taffy Floral
Calligraphy: Meant to be Calligraphy

The inspiration for this wedding suite was drawn from movie posters. Weddings could feel like putting on a movie or show. There were so many moving parts to the production from the officiant, caterers, floral designers, photographers, etc. This wedding suite was a play on that concept. The save the date card was like a sneak peak teaser for the invitation and the invitation listed out all the key elements.

This suite was entirely letterpressed and printed on 100% cotton paper. This suite easily matched with any color palette for a wedding, which made it versatile since the colors for the wedding were not yet selected when designing the suite. To add a splash of color, the vintage stamps had a purple theme to them and a modern style calligraphy was used for the envelope to compliment the modern style of this invite.

We had a great time styling the shoot using eucalyptus and other greenery to compliment the suite. Taffy Floral styled the flowers while Rachel Lynn Photography took the photos. The calligraphy on the envelopes was done by Meant to be Calligraphy.

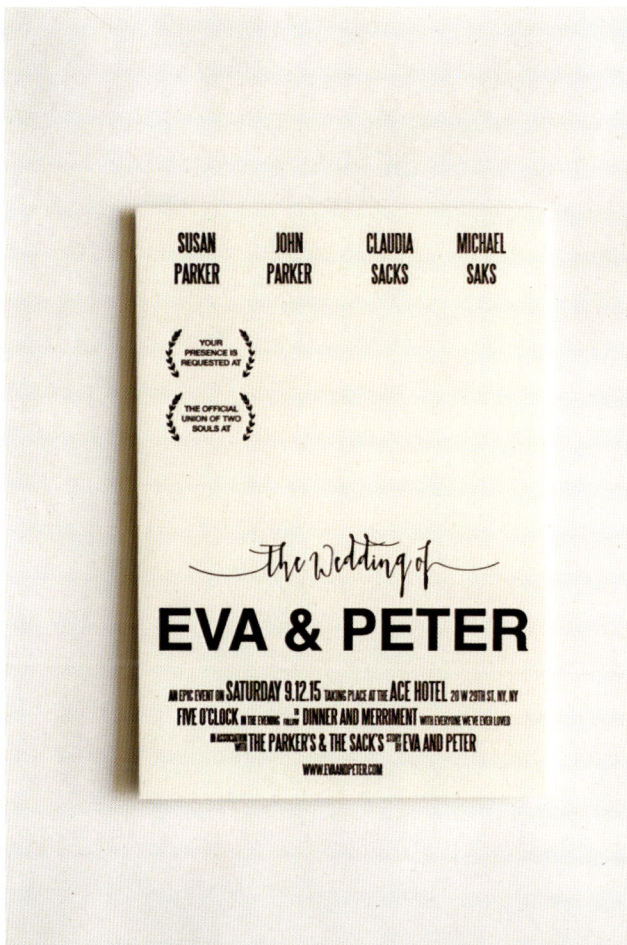

Rebecca Collection Letterpress Wedding Suite

Design Agency: Miks Letterpress + Designer: Mariko Iwata
Stationery photos: Rachel Lynn Photography
Floral: Taffy Floral
Calligraphy: Meant to be Calligraphy

This wedding suite was done for a couple who wanted a modern look to their wedding invitation. They wanted something simple, masculine and clean. They also wanted a hint of color and the boxy look was the right touch for their wedding suite. This suite was printed using soy-based ink and paper that was tree free and made from 100% cotton linters, which were left over from the textile industry. It was acid free, recyclable, biodegradable and elemental chlorine free.

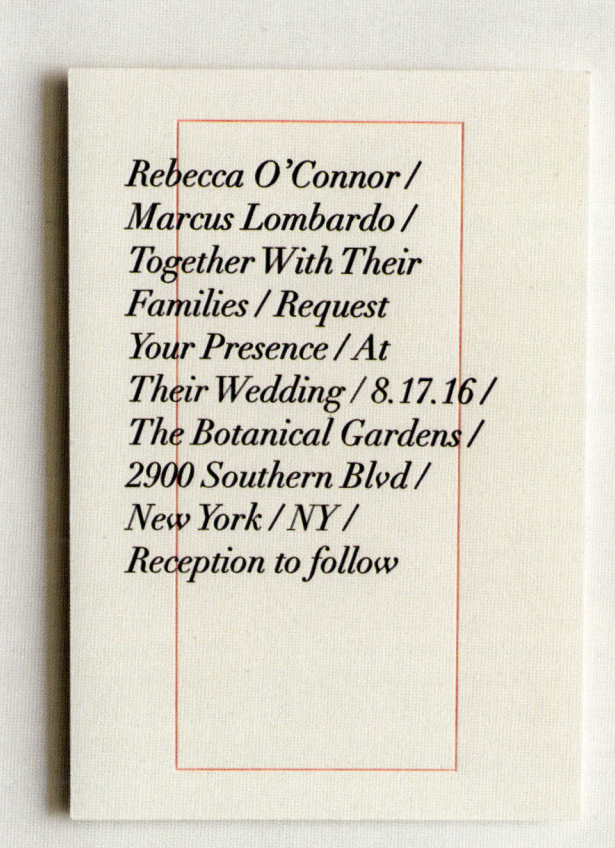

D & U Wedding Stationery

Designer: Doreen Baldauf-Uhlmann
Photography: Doreen Baldauf-Uhlmann, Marlén Mieth

With its combination of a clean font and hand lettering, the stationery reflected how well the couple's different characters fit together – he was very organized and she was the creative chaos. Together they formed a symbiosis. The idea for this creative concept was born out of her interest in typography and his fondness for her hand lettering work.

They both had a dream of a summer countryside wedding with modern details. The color of the small church was the inspiration for the coloring of the stationery. To fit a modern style, each paper item only used white lettering against a background of a single color. The layout of the stationery was deliberately kept very clean and simple to focus attention on the hand lettering.

The inspiration for this design came from the urban environment, for example lettering in old-fashioned type on buildings, and from ephemera such as magazines and newspapers from the 1920's to the 1950's.

The wedding favors were also made using typography, printed on small wooden panels. The idea for this came during Doreen's four month journey around Southeast Asia. Every week she would draw one letter on a postcard and send it to her fiancé. Finally, 62 different letters were created in this way. Every guest received a personalized wood panel with their printed initial.

The wedding theme was "Hand in Hand ein Leben lang" which meant holding hands forever. It was communicated in several ways: printed in the invitation as well in the ceremony program, laser-cut from wood and mounted in the reception room, and finally engraved in the wedding rings.

As a result, a complete set – invitation, menu, program, signs, tags, seating plan and favors – was designed and produced, using over 90 different letterings.

· The design draft

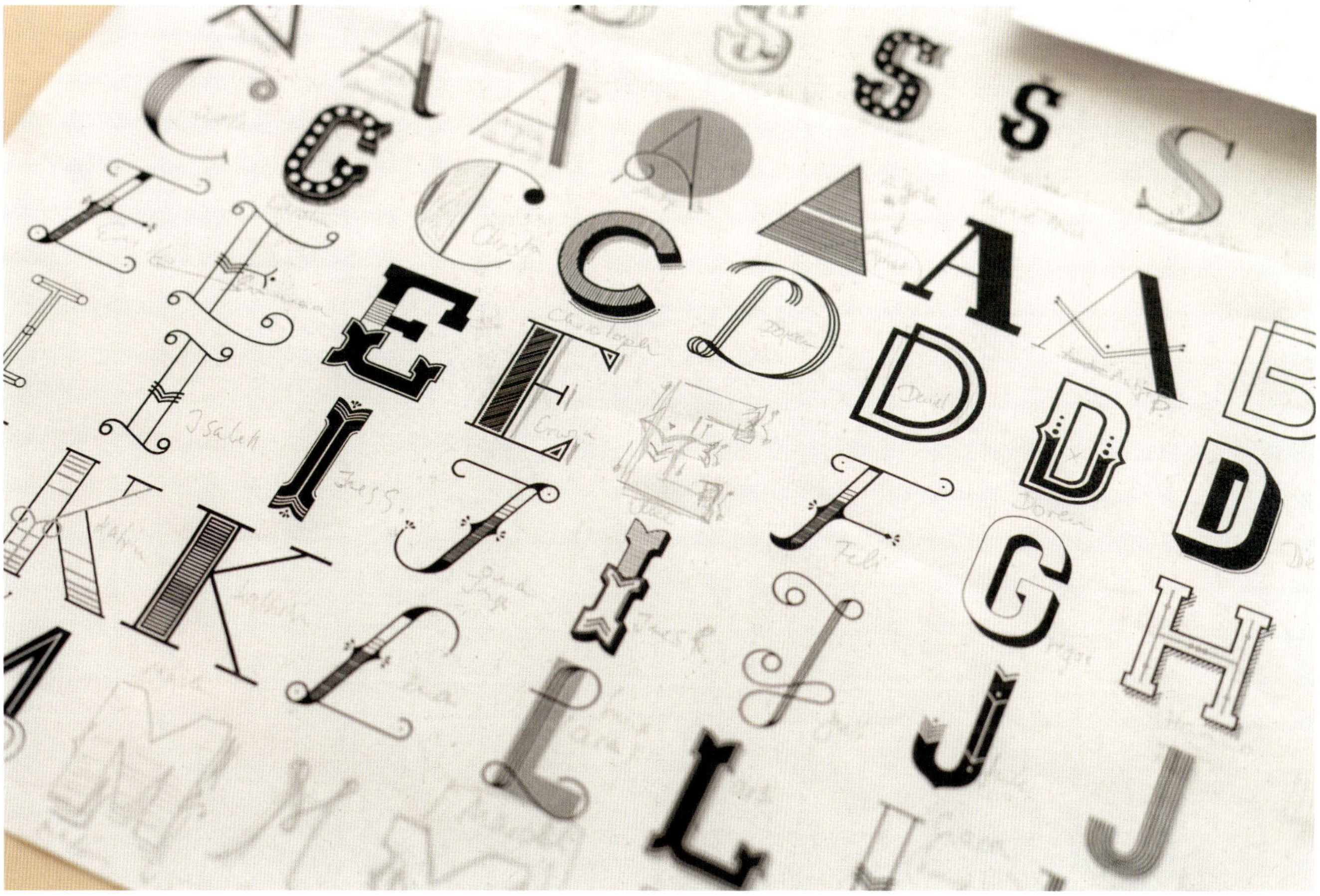

· The invitation

· on-location

· Thank-You Card

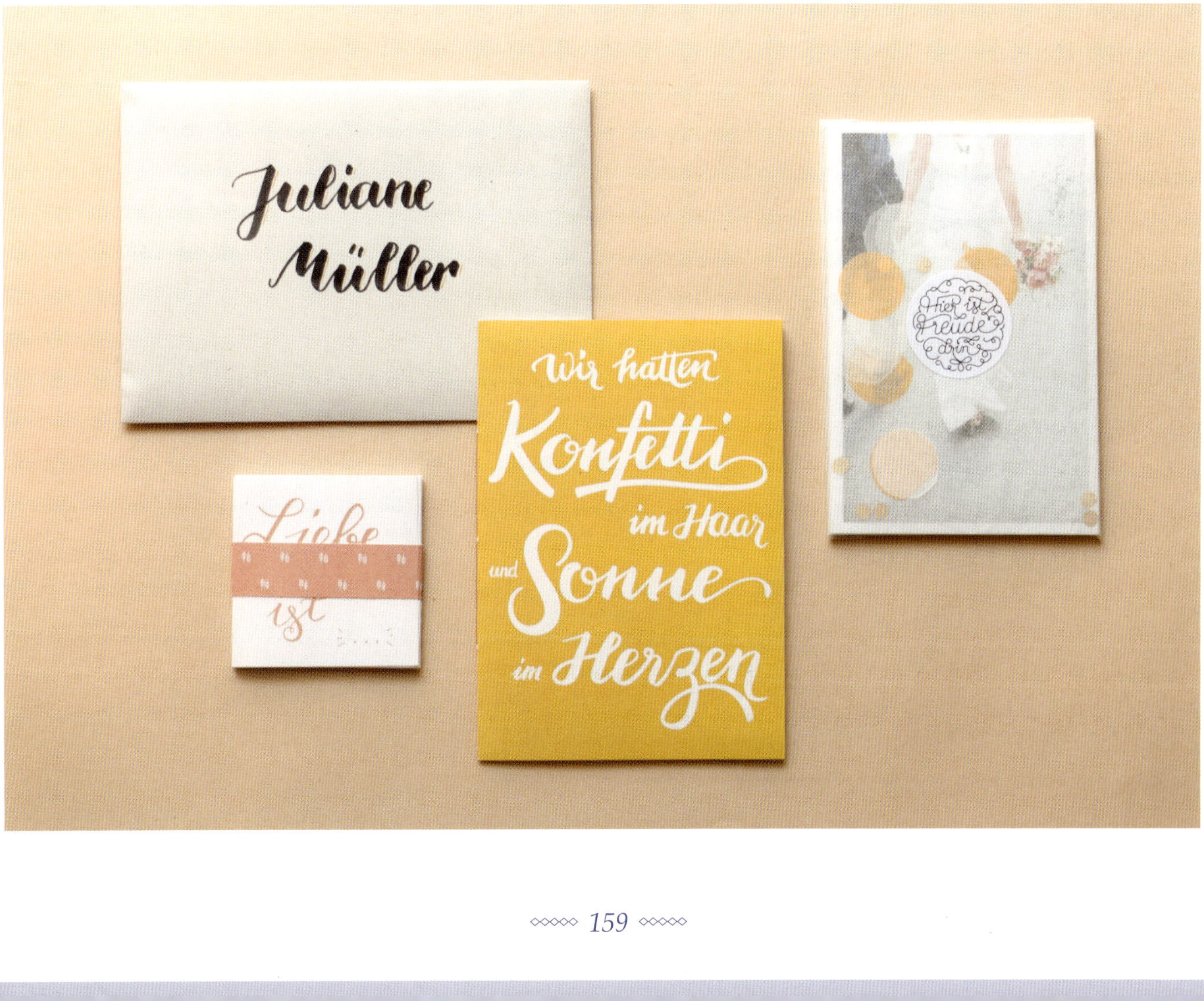

Wedding Invitation Set

Design Agency: FØLSOM Studio   *Client:* Imprimerie du Marais, La Belle Histoire
Photography: FØLSOM Studio   *Copyright:* 2015 © FØLSOM Studio

Imprimerie du Marais was well known for its high quality and very refined printing services. In 2015, the company created La Belle Histoire, an e-shop selling set of wedding invitations. The brand confided us the artistic direction and the graphic design of one of these sets, inspired by the world of fashion and luxury. Thus we experimented the expression of gesture in an artistic way, using spray techniques on paper that we digitized and reworked. Moreover, we designed a unique ampersand in order to express the beauty of the union of two lovers, drawing smooth curves and moves that we can also identify in haute-couture creations. The set was printed with pink gold foil on a night blue paper and a pink iridescent paper to create a strong contrast and highlight the shining flakes.

François & Kelly

Design Agency: Atelier BangBang & Studio Caserne
Designer: Léo Breton-Allaire
Client: François & Kelly   Printer: Simon Lalibrté

François and Kelly are two very good friends. For their wedding gift, we give them a formal exercise about their names' forts letters. In order to invite their friends and relatives, it has been printed by screen process printing for 200 copies of all pieces, with love. The kit is composed of: Invitations, response cards, envelopes, gift box, candy bags and coasters. White and gold have been chosen by the couple to be their thematic colors. The metallic pigment from the solvent ink provides a light reflexion evoking strength and elegance.

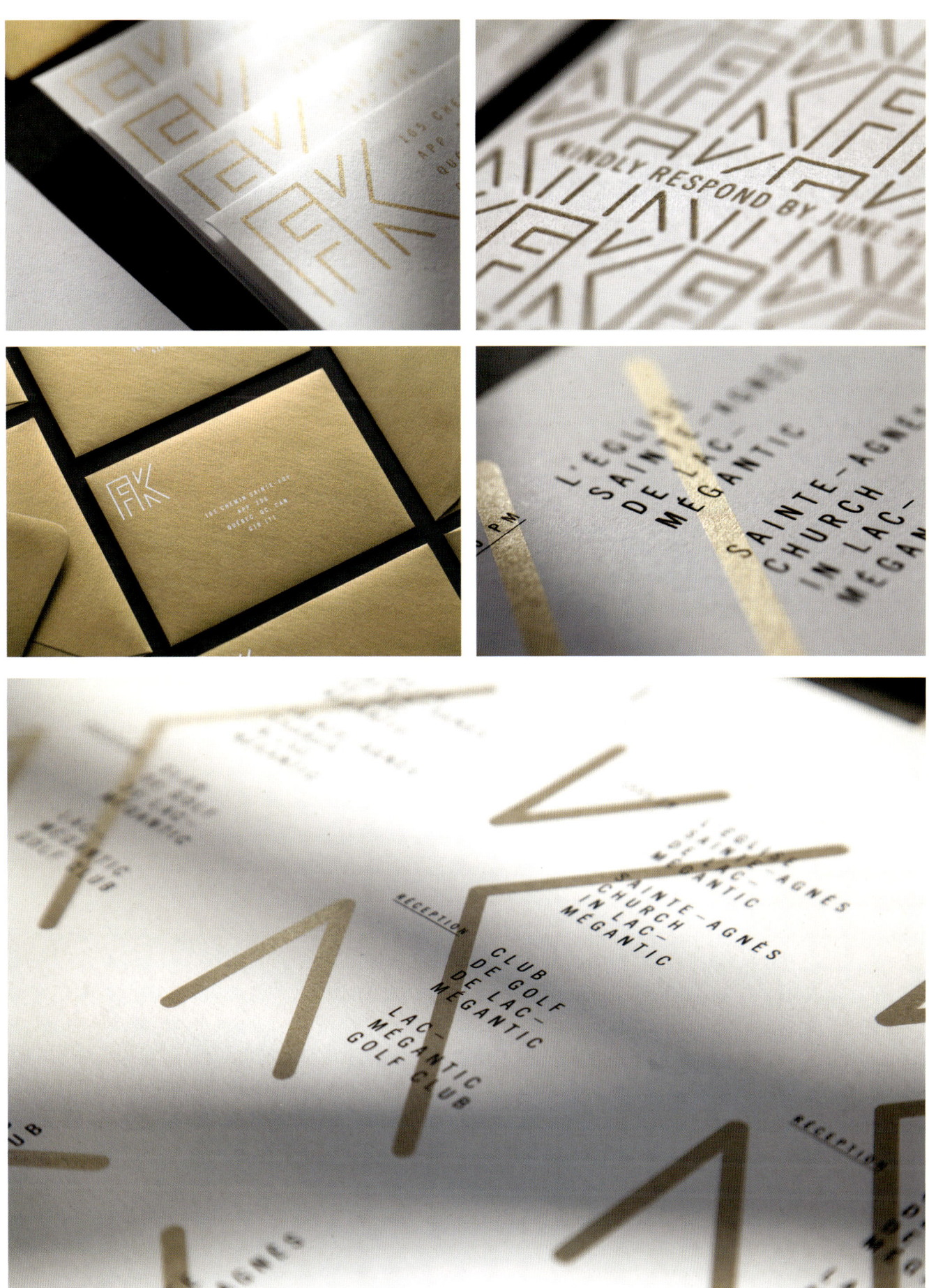

Maritime Wedding Series

Designer: MARTSON (Marta Chmielarz)

Because I'm very into maritime themes, I design wedding series in nautical style for Studio Brzoza based in Poznań/Poland. The effects of our collaboration are: menu cards, vignettes, a guestbook, tables marking, gratitude notes and alcohol labels.

The flat design with geometric elements, narrow color ranges is working well with sailing atmosphere. The invitations are designed in various styles — depending on what budget you are disposing — you can choose variant with laser cut or tied with a thin string. All the elements are available on Studio Brzoza's website.

Luxury Wedding Invitation for Cat-lover

Design Agency: In The Castle Design   Creative Director: Hironobu Jyounai   Photographer: Hironobu Jyounai   Client: Kohei & Natsuki   Illustrator: Hironobu Jyounai

Letterpress, gold foil and custom die cut invitation, features a cute cat illustration. These gold leaf place cards are easy to make and add the perfect touch to your Thanksgiving dinner table!

Erickson Wedding Invitation

Designer: Caitlin Workman

This is an event and invitation design for Heather and Taylor Erickson. This alluring and distinctive system was inspired by modern sensibilities. Gold metallic ink was used to create consistency and sophistication through ornate elegance. A self mailing RSVP card was designed to eliminate the need for additional materials and allowed for a cost-effective, one-color print production. The intricate design reflected whimsy, timelessness and pastoral elements aligning with the thematic direction. Ornaments were inspired by art deco line work to resemble lace, defining a delicate and dynamic design.

M+M Invitations

Designer: Mustaali Raj   Printing Agency: JukeBox Print

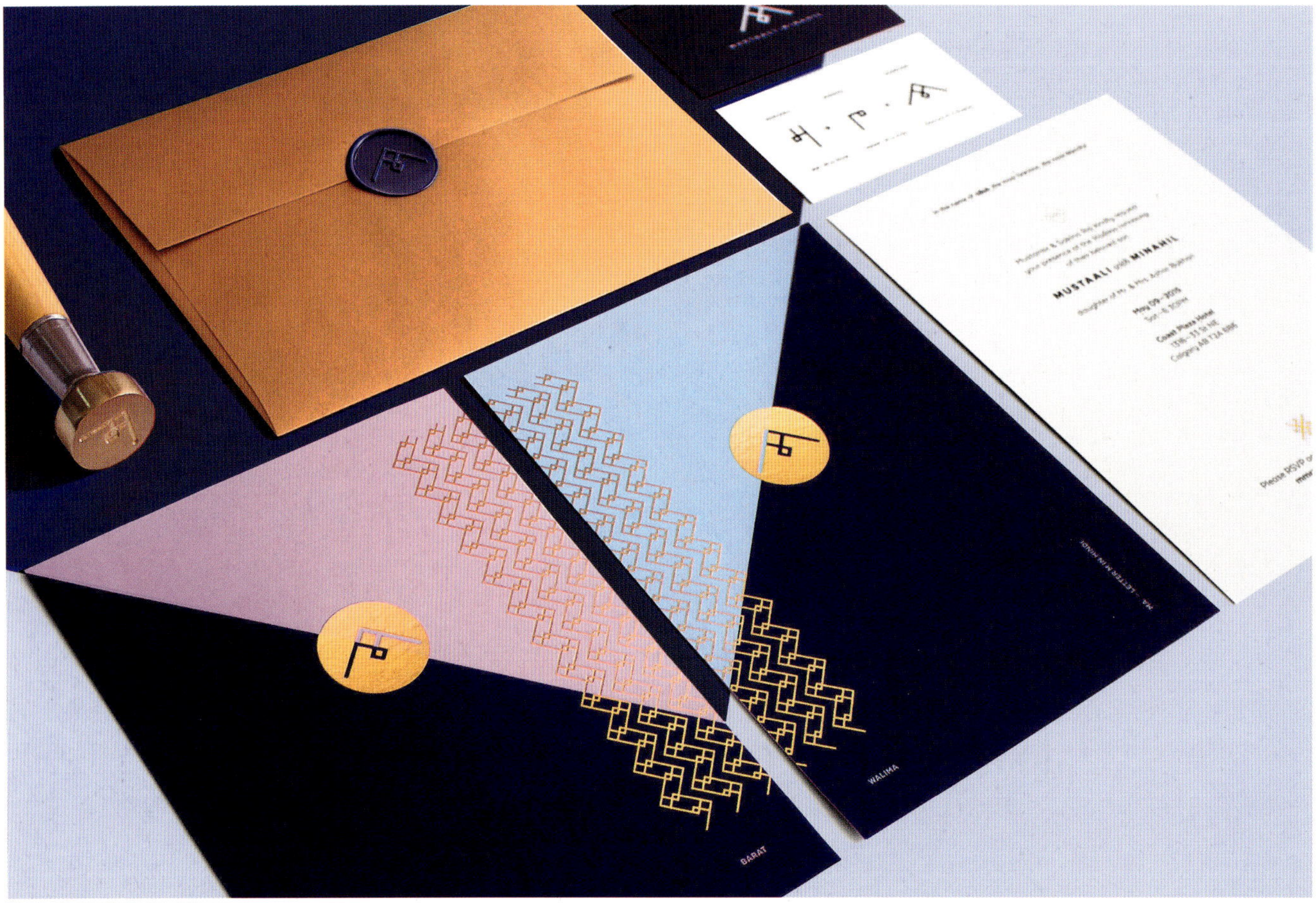

These personal wedding invitations are designed for Mustaali and Minahil's wedding. The primary logo is derived from the letter M in Hindi (representing Mustaali's Indian heritage) and Urdu (representing Minahil's Pakistani heritage) respectively. Soft colors and gold foil paired with geometric layouts bring a contemporary flair to a traditional Indian wedding.

The cards are made for two separate events, one hosted by the bride and the other hosted by the groom. The diagonals play an important role in the layout as they reveal and conceal different parts of the logo. The central seal reveals the M in Hindi for the groom's event (Walima) and the M in Urdu for the bride's event (Barat). This represents the coming together of two cultures yet celebrating their unique backgrounds.

Wedding Invitation for Juan y Alicia

Designer: Romualdo Faura   Illustrator: Romualdo Faura
Photography: Hugo Blanes

The idea when designing this invitation is to combine the tradition (had to include all data that usually have a classic wedding invitation) with a modern touch, based on pictographic style illustrations.

In each sheet of the invitation all important events that will place at the wedding are illustrated. On the one hand, it contains the introduction of the bride and groom, their parents (which in Spain are usually introduced in the invitations), the Church, the date, the place of feasting, even the bank account number to receive gifts.

It is elected an elongated format to view all the small illustrations when the guests open the invitation.

Black and gold are chosen to intensify the idea of the tradition and classicism because these two colors provide a good contrast.

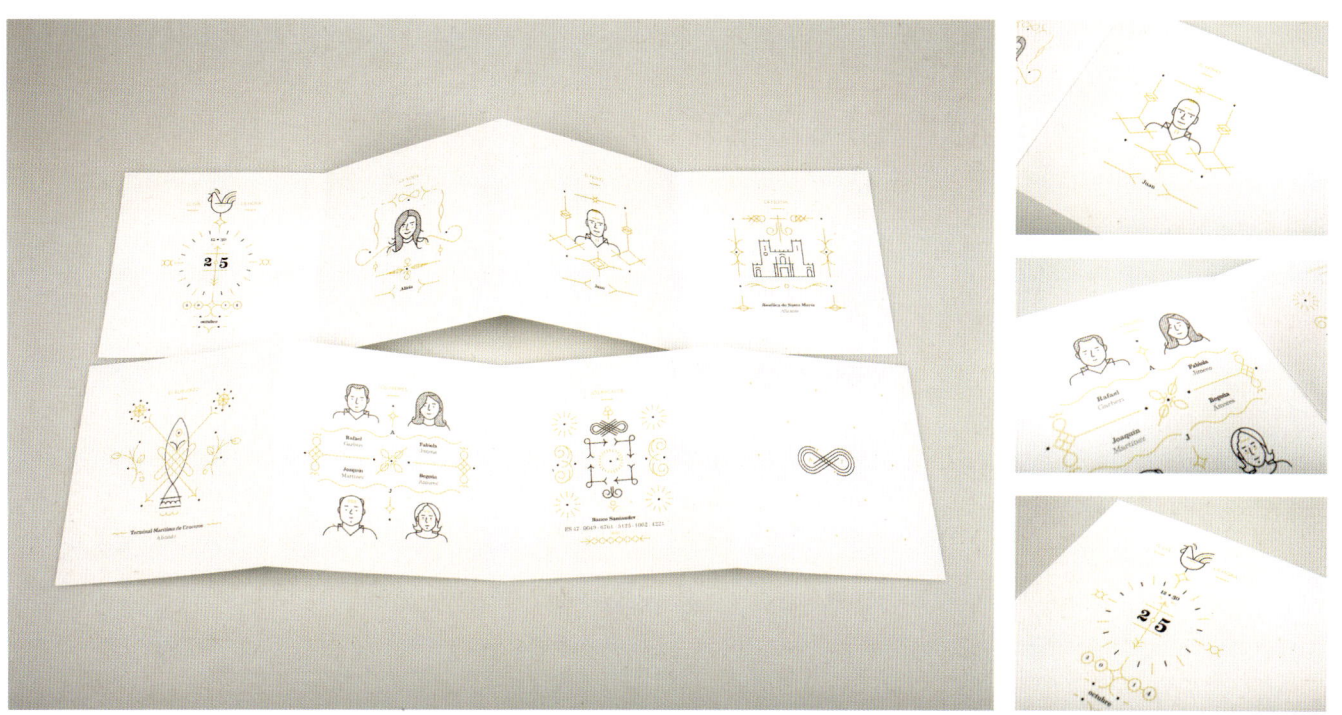

Wedding Invitation for M&J

Designer: Lívia Vernarská   Client: Matúš & Janka   Illustrator: Lívia Vernarská

This project was created for my brother Matúš and his longtime girlfriend and best friend Janka. When they asked me to create this wedding invitation, I was delighted. They are my favorite couple, so I looked for something special for them. Something they would love and at the same time there would be a part of them in this work. I chose the simple, pure and modern style. The package contained the wedding invitation, the invitation to a wedding table, wedding place card, the envelope and special additional paper with one of the best known and the most beautiful verses about love, The First Letter of St. Paul to the Corinthians.

This wedding invitation had dimensions 100mm×145mm. It contained the most important information like the date and the time of the wedding, the wedding venue and some additional text. I chose soft pastel colors and the combination of white, cream and different shades of blue.

Invitation to the wedding table and special paper with verses from the Holy Bible have dimensions 80mm×80mm and 100mm×290mm. I chose black Sans serif font — it looked beautiful and it had a good readability at the same time.

What cannot be omitted was that all this work was printed on the nice textured watercolor paper with weight 160 gm. The whole package was tied with jute and packed to the envelope, which was made from the craft material. On the top of the back side was the written verses from the Hymn of Love in handwriting: "But now faith, hope, love, abide these three; but the greatest of these is love." 1 Corinthians, 13,13.

The project was created in the conception of simplicity, flowers, pastel colors and beautiful high quality material. I wanted the whole project to be not only visually pleasant but also with a special spirit.

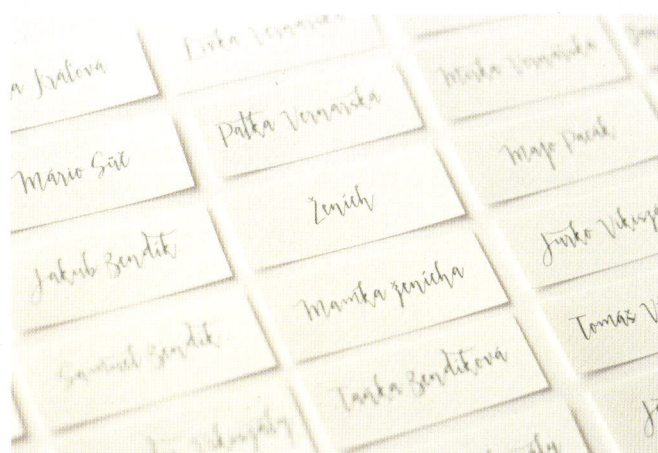

FUN

Design Agency: Convictus   Creative Director: Pedro Sousa   Designer: Filipa Sousa
Client: Sofia & Bruno   Illustrator: Filipa Sousa   Photographer: Pedro Sousa

The invitation FUN is characterized by fun, colorful and full of movement.

With horizontal crease the invitation is defined by a graph with the couple's names and inside with a graphic composition of all the event information.

177

Júlia & Ricardo

Design Agency: Convictus   *Creative Director:* Pedro Sousa   *Designer:* Filipa Sousa
Client: Júlia & Ricardo   *Illustrator:* Filipa Sousa   *Photographer:* Pedro Sousa

This is an invitation inspired by the vibrant colors of the farms in May. It is an invitation leaflet which is featured by the couple's names and inside a graphic composition of all the information relating to the wedding.

Susana & Pedro

Design Agency: Convictus   Creative Director: Pedro Sousa   Designer: Filipa Sousa
Client: Susana & Pedro   Illustrator: Filipa Sousa   Photographer: Pedro Sousa

It is an invitation inspired by the theme of the sea. The iconography of the invitation is based on the elements of the sea, the ocean, fishing vessels, crustaceans...

AC

Designer: María Hernández   Client: Almudena y Cesar
Illustrator: María Hernández

To transmit the idea of union, I created a series of patterns that developed straightly from the first letters of the couple's first names. The invitation was a metaphor of what all the bride and the groom will create during their lives.

The Year in Love & Thanks

Design Agency: ORIGIN.DESIGN studio   Creative Director: Rui Juan Lin

We would like to deliver our sincere messages of Love & Appreciation to those who have received our wedding invitations. In order to create a joyful + pleasant atmosphere on a 2-dimensional greeting card, we played around with the typography and hand-made textures. We tied our cards with the strings of twine, and created our own gold-stamping plate for an extra touch of elegant feel.

Wedding Anniversary Papercut

Artist: Julene Harrison

This pretty wedding anniversary piece features the initials and a portrait of the couple. All of my work is designed using Adobe Photoshop, then printed and cut by hand.

Papercut Wedding Artwork

Artist: Julene Harrison

This large 20" × 20" heart-shaped piece was commissioned by the couple to celebrate their wedding. It was made up of pertinent dates, places and motifs that told the story of their relationship. When making a piece like this one the hardest element was making everything fit together. The back of the cockerel and the London underground sign both made for useful shapes with composing the overall heart outline.

London Themed Papercut Wedding Invitation

Artist: Julene Harrison

I only created the original papercut for my clients. They arranged the duplication. I would send them either a photo of the piece which they could have printed or letterpressed. Or a vector file, the type used by laser-cutting machines. They would then send this file to a laser-cutter for reproduction. In both cases I would post them the original piece to keep and frame.

Food Inspired Papercut Wedding Invitation

Artist: Julene Harrison

A food themed papercut that was commissioned as a wedding gift, photographed with the paper scraps and the scalpel.

Papercut Wedding Invitation

Artist: Julene Harrison

For this wedding invitation the client wanted all the details to be included on the papercut itself. The challenge was to keep the piece visually interesting as it was in reality just lines of text. Due to the nature of papercut every letter had to be attached to something, you had to find ways to "hide" this, so it was not all underlined and mixing positive and negative lines of text.

Luggage Tag Save the Date

Design Agency: Atheneum Creative   Creative Director: Melissa Broderick
Designer: Melissa Broderick   Photographer: Chelsea Davis
Client: Mary and Kosta

Mary and Kosta were getting married in Greece and wanted to set the travel theme off with a luggage tag. We printed real luggage tags with the custom monogram and inserted the details. The tag was mailed in a box with the inside cover showing a map of the location. A simple design, a simple save the date, but the couple really wanted to set the tone with this first impression to all their guests who would be traveling.

Brantley

Design Agency: Atheneum Creative   Creative Director: Melissa Broderick
Designer: Melissa Broderick   Client: Caroline and Edward
Photographer: Chelsea Davis

Caroline and Edward were having a winter wedding and wanted an invitation that would speak to the soft, quiet and calm nature of winter. We used soft greys and whites with letterpress and foil to achieve this feeling.

Folder Wedding Invitation for Jandira & Pitter

Design Agency: etc & co   Designer: Filipa Sobral & Maria Moura
Client: Jandira & Pitter

Being a young couple, Jandira and Pitter asked for an invitation that was romantic, with floral and fruit elements without being too classic. They wanted something youthful and fresh with the color scheme of white and silver.

Not being able to use color, we decided to create a laser cut pattern of leaves and fruits with the couple's names blind embossed. This allowed the invitation keep white as the dominant color, only using the silver foil for the inside text. The invitation itself had a very simple construction – it was basically folded two times not even needing an envelope as it was very important for us and the client to showcase the intricate laser cut pattern. Although it was quite subtle, a lot of fruits – that were later used for decorating the wedding venue – were featured in the design.

Inside, the invitation relied on typography. In order to have a better readability and to keep the design young and modern, the matte silver foil was used instead of the usual shinny foil.

It was quite a challenge to design from the original briefing as we had to include the floral elements, fruits and typography, and we had to keep it white and silver only and use laser cut, blind embossing and silver foil. The main concern was to make sure the final result was elegant, modern and youthful, as well as romantic and using all of the elements mentioned above. In the end, not using color was actually one of the best ways to achieve this look – and although it was from 2012, it remained timeless and still a favorite today.

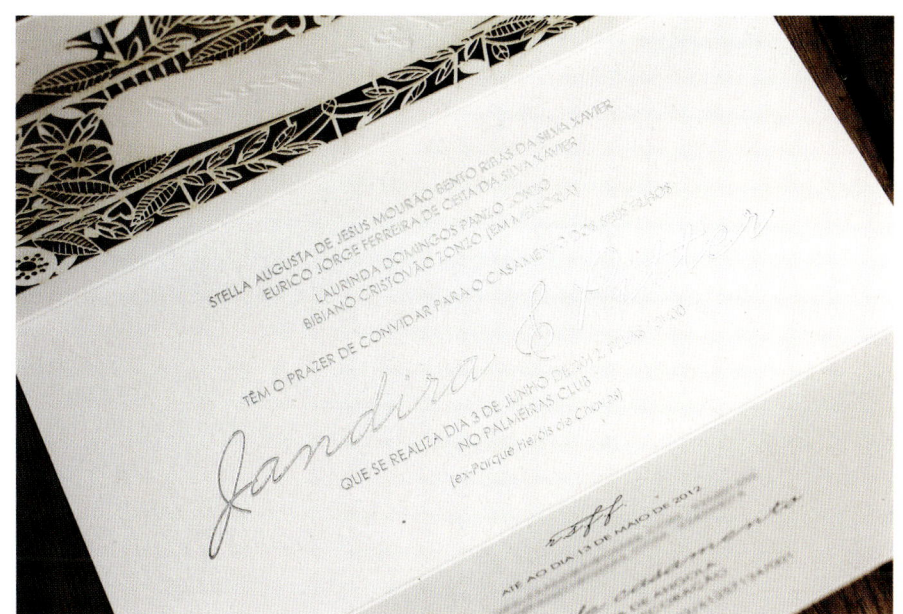

R & R Wedding Invite

Designer: Rola Khadra   Client: Rola and Rami   Illustrator: Rola Khadra

R&R Wedding Invite was a personal project I worked on for my wedding in Mykonos, Greece. After choosing the destination and venue, I wanted to design a wedding invite that was special, memorable and reflecting the mood and colors of the venue.

I wanted my invite to be interactive and sweet. What's sweeter than chocolate?

First I created a simple logo with our initials (Rola and Rami) and printed the invite artwork on the brown recycled paper. Then I bought plenty of chocolate bars and removed their original wrapping to replace it with mine.

The rest of the chocolate package was handmade one by one using the brown organza ribbon, brown rope and lace. I then printed the invitees' names on small tags and attached them to the invite using metal hooks.

All our friends went crazy over the invite. They posted photos on social media and thanked us for all the efforts we put into them.

Weddings are special and what you're left with are sweet memories, so we want to make them last.

Kirstin & Pablo

Design Agency: The Pick of the Crab   Designer: Paula Zuñiga Garcés
Illustrator: Paula Zuñiga Garcés   Photography: Paula Zuñiga Garcés

We were called to design the wedding invitation to the Kirstin & Pablo Marriage in Punta de Lobos, Chile. Our proposal was based in a fresh image, using humor and ludic objects for creating a funny atmosphere for the guests.

We created an invitation that turned into a map that indicated the road to arrive to the party and simple graphic pieces for the menu, the locations where each guest was gonna be seated, message cards for the guest to leave message to the new couple, souvenirs of the party, etc. All conceptualized, designed and illustrated thinking to evoke characteristic beach and ocean iconography. To achieve this we created ludic illustrations of the surroundings of Punta de Lobos beach, fishes, sirens, sea stars, ships, sea lions and several beautiful and funny illustrations to make everyone happy.

VI GIFTER OSS

OG HAR DERFOR GLEDEN
AV Å INVITERE

★ til vielse ★

Amy & Hanker Wedding Visual Identity and Invitation Design /
Aldine & Ned Wedding Identity /
Mayra & Jorge Wedding Identity /
T+S Wedding Invitation /
Wang & Cheng Wedding Invitation /
Cecely & Pasquale Wedding Stationaries /
Moon & Sun /
Wedding Typography /
N & P /
Bo & Oak Wedding Invitation Card

. . . .

Traditional with a Twist
Chapter Five

Amy & Hanker Wedding Visual Identity and Invitation Design

Design Agency: Rose QR LIN   Designer: Rose QR LIN   Client: Hanker Lv Zheng
Photographer: Rose QR LIN

Amy and Hanker were keen to have a wedding ceremony featuring white for their pure love, while keeping a minimalist style on their invitation and main visual.

The wedding VI design featured the groom and bride's name initials, and the color palette of the wedding ceremony and applications were also carefully planned. Common wedding elements and white lilies were designed with a contemporary aesthetic approach of a metallic gradient finishing. In addition, the wedding poster and invitation were offset printed with silver foil stamping on the premium GF Smith paper stock.

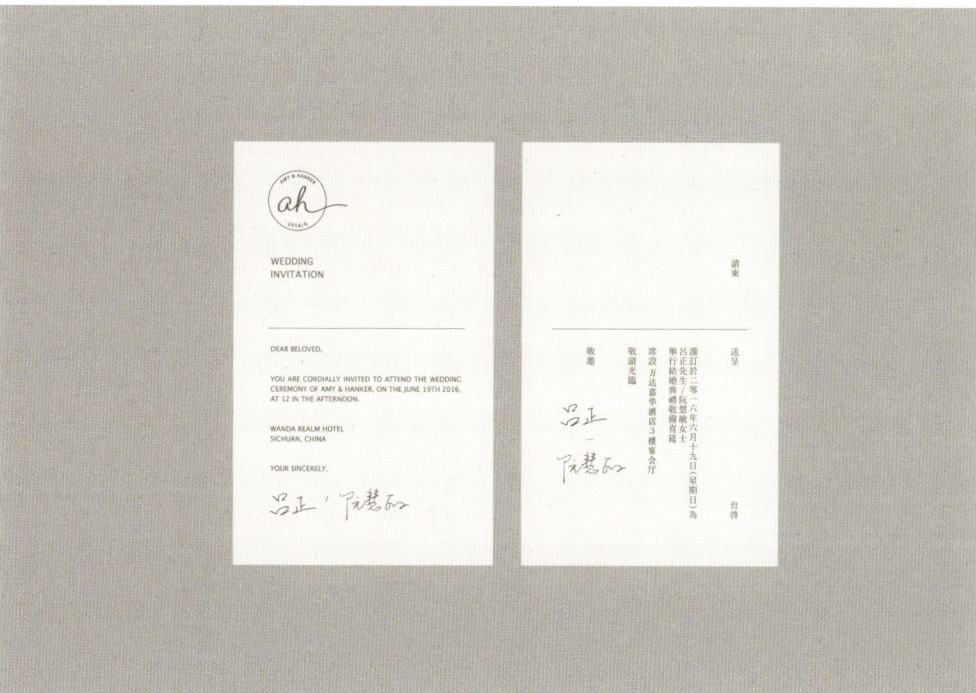

 # *Aldine & Ned Wedding Identity*

Designer: Mayra Monobe   Client: Aldine Mizushima and Ned Ashmore

This Wedding Identity was for a British-Brazilian couple that got married in a paradisiacal beach in Brazil. The project took in consideration the origins of the couple and the fact that they got married in an informal ceremony. It had to have lots of information for people travelling from other countries to a small town in Brazil, so it included a small booklet with maps, hotels and general travelling information.

The overall style was based on the couple's personalities. Simple yet elegant, and icons were added to be easily understandable by guests from different countries.

Other elements, such as fans for the guests and dinner menus were further additions to the identity for the wedding day.

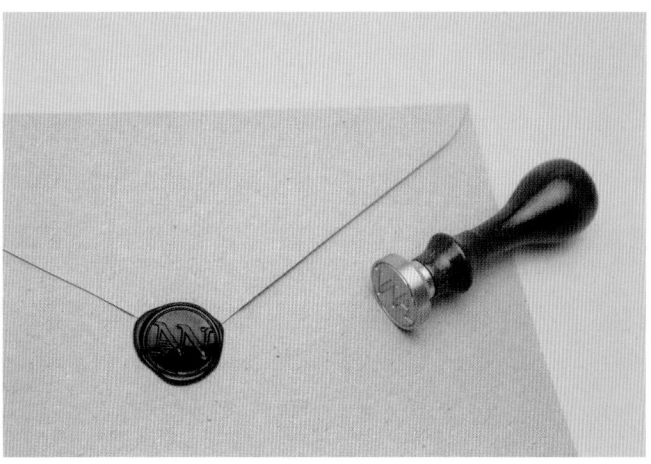

Mayra & Jorge Wedding Identity

Designer: Mayra Monobe   Client: Mayra Monobe & Jorge Alavedra

This Wedding Identity was for a Spanish-Brazilian couple with very different personalities. The overall idea was to use two different typefaces — a serif and a sans-serif — to communicate each person's differences, yet complementing each other.

Since guests were coming from all over the world, different elements were created in order to personalize each invitation and include only the relevant information for each guest. The elements included the invite with all relevant info, a booklet with two covers to explain Jorge and Mayra's lives until they met, gift cards with photos of the honeymoon destination, hotel and travelling info sheets, translations and thank you notes.

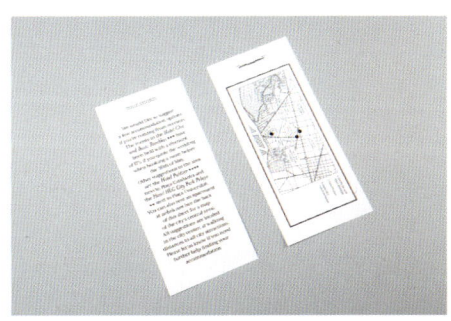

T+S Wedding Invitation

Design Agency: Kristin Klette   Designer: Kristin Klette
Client: Stig Ove Hol and Tonje Stenseth

All elements connected to the wedding have the same design – black text with graphic elements and headings in pink and green on white. At the party, the design shifts into darker and slightly less solemn – the bar menu is in dark brown with the negative design in white.

Wang & Cheng Wedding Invitation

Design Agency: Abingo Wang Design Affairs   Designer: Ting Bin Wang
Client: Mr. and Mrs. Wang   Photographer: Show Leejuan

Eastern wedding invitation design tends to have the fixed convention. I want to break away from the existed design style. Therefore, in terms of color, I avoid red and gold and choose a peachy-pink color card with silver foil stamping, which symbolizes sweetness; and then I reinterpret the traditional pattern of "Dragon Phoenix Auspicious" and modernize it, so that the complex Eastern traditional pattern is presented by simplified lines. In its typeface I also echo it with decorative lines in an attempt to flip the conventional Eastern format into an innovative wedding design.

Cecely & Pasquale Wedding Stationaries

Design Agency: The Moon and Back   Designer: Cavi Chen
Client: Cecely & Pasquale   Illustrator: Cavi Chen

Cecely is Chinese and Pasquale is Italian. They want to celebrate their wedding with the theme of mix and matching these two cultures. The idea is to blend together the different elements of their nationalities.

Cecely loves traditional Chinese painting and she wants to share the happiness of the marriage to her passed away teacher as well. Both of their paintings are featured into the invitation as part of the key visual throughout the collection.

At the front of the invitation, parts of the Chinese and Italian patterns are embossed and applied with hot foil stamping effect. Together, they create a unique visual impact. The patterns synchronise well with the white color because of its rich details. The names of the couple and the word " 囍 " are the only objects with color, which lead the addressee to focus on the purpose of the invitation at the first sight.

" 囍 " means combining two joyful people and families together, in other word, double happiness. This Chinese character is generally not used in a text but as a graphic sign only.

Moon & Sun

Designer: Wildan Ilham Mahibuddin   Client: Dena & Dhika
Photographer: Wildan Ilham Mahibuddin

Moon & Sun is the invitation for my beloved sister's wedding. Based on dreamy pink, white and glamorous gold, I come up with a modern piece that exudes the heart-warming vibe when moon meets the sun. Unique floral elements bear a subtle art deco reference, making the design stand out from traditional wedding invitations.

Wedding Typography

Designer: Elena Greenforg   Illustrator: Elena Greenforg

The style of the wedding typography primarily relied on the entire theme of the event: iridescence, brightness and lightness. In the second place the entire selection of color solutions and its diversity reflected the newlyweds themselves, who were not used to miss, and their lively, loud and cheerful nature.

The entire project consisted of a number of variations: the invitations (the idea belonged to the couple themselves), which differed in sizes and styles, numbers at the tables, seating cards with the names of guests, cards of the event, letters of appreciation, additional elements such as envelopes and covers.

Lightweight, childishness and most importantly the variety of colors distinguished this design; it reflected a sense of celebration and joy that the whole wedding was riddled.

N&P

Designer: Constança Soromenho

Nadia and Pedro wanted nothing less from their big day, than for it to be a fun and creative one, where guests could take part in the celebration. The wedding suite had to match that so, alongside with the invitation, guests received RSVP card that they could fill with their own song suggestion. Also there were pins for the best men and bridesmaids, and disposable cameras in every table with messages encouraging guests to have fun and capture unforgettable moments.

This wedding suite was the perfect fusion between the bride's ideas and wishes and the designer's inputs and creations.

Bo & Oak Wedding Invitation Card

Design Agency: Wide & Narrow Co., Ltd   Creative Director: Kanwee Harichanwong
Art Director: Poomruethai Suebsantiwongse   Designer: Poomruethai Suebsantiwongse
Client: Narintra & Chayanarong Sutthinark

The Bo & Oak invitation design expresses its harmony through the symbols of their love story. The big oak tree represents the man who has a strong heart and long-lasting love. The bride's name, "Bo", has a meaning in Thai as ribbon. Through this simple illustration, the ribbon is wrapping around the oak tree with the love she has for him. The material design for this project includes: wedding invitation card, engagement invitation card, envelope, wax stamp and map.

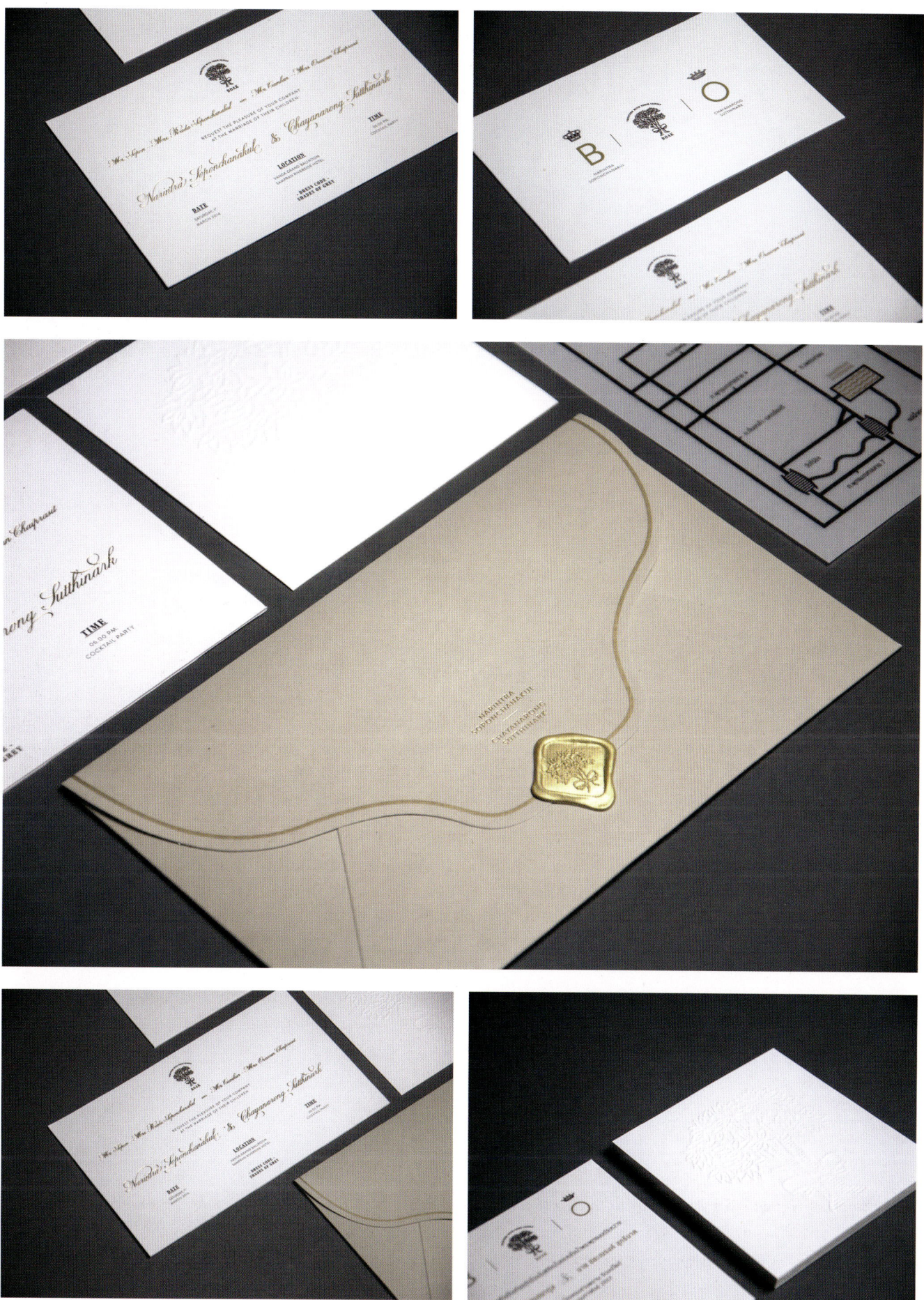

D & K Wedding Invitation /
1920s Deco /
Game of Thrones /
Juan & Laura Wedding Invitation /
Paul & Kat Wedding Invitation Suite /
T & P /
Ana & Sergio /
A Wedding Invitation /
N & M Wedding Cards /
Ola & Daniel Wedding Invitation /
Wedding Invitation /
Wedding Invites /

. . . .

Vintage Inspired
Chapter Six

D & K Wedding Invitation

Design Agency: Bureau Rabensteiner   Client: Klaus Ehrenfried

Shabby chic with a squeeze of lemon – this was how we would describe the stationery design for the wedding of Daniela & Klaus. The ceremony and festivities took place in a beautiful location in Mallorca, Spain. To design a wedding invitation was a "first" for us which we really enjoyed. Instead of just working with the typography and paper we decided to put our focus very much on the still life photography. It was an uncommon way for this kind of stationery, but we wanted to create a "Message in the Bottle" key visual to get people in the right mood and excited about D&K's Special Day weeks before the wedding.

THE SWEETEST DAY

D&K

Daniela Klaus

1920s Deco

Design Agency: Atelier Isabey

This invitation suite took the Art Deco style to the next level with high fashion inspired black and gold. Printed in dazzling gold foil on the thick black stock, the invitation was evocative of a dramatic piece of costume jewelry or couture accessory, a look that truly embodied the vision the couple were looking to achieve. All pieces in the suite were printed in gold foil on luxury stock and envelopes.

Game of Thrones

Design Agency: Atelier Isabey

Like many, we at Atelier Isabey are huge fans of the acclaimed HBO series Game of Thrones (based on the R.R. Martin's fantasy novels). We want to do a special tribute to this spellbinding series and the unforgettable characters whose paths are intricately woven together to create a truly epic story. As designers, what we particularly love is how the creative team of the show brought to life every aspect with meticulous attention to detail. Every house, unique culture and land in Game of Thrones has its own particular look and feel which is unlike any other.

With that in mind, we decide to celebrate the new season by bringing our Atelier Isabey aesthetic and creativity and create five looks that are inspired by some of our favorite Game of Thrones characters and families. The invitation suites are designed and printed with only the finest quality papers, artisanal letterpress and foil as well as laser cutting techniques.

Juan & Laura
Wedding Invitation

Design Agency: El Calotipo   Designer: Nelson Moya   Client: Juan & Laura
Photography: Carla Nicolás

These were Juan and Laura's wedding invites. They came to our studio to delegate the design and print services but before we got some guidelines to follow in.

Designed in 2 colors and an unusual format (10 cm × 15 cm), the invitation card was printed with the art of handmade typography from printing plates on thick paper (700 gsm). Each envelope was decorated with a printed label with same colors and die cut to give a stamp appearance.

Paul & Kat Wedding Invitation Suite

Designer & Calligrapher: Pauline A. Ibarra, Happy Hands Project
Client: Paul Rodulfo Imperial & Katherine May Rances
Photographer: Mango Red Studios

The design brief I had received for this invitation suite was to design something very classy and elegant, similar to the movie "Meet Joe Black". It was a perfect excuse to indulge myself with a classic chick flick, and that's exactly what I did! I envisioned it to be a black tie event (sans the peanut butter), very formal and upscale. Using a simple black and white palette, I incorporated baroque-style elements and a modern pointed pen calligraphy script, which resulted in a suite that embodied sophistication and romance.

T & P

Design Agency: Hoja Studio   Designer: Elizabet Corsaro   Client: Tamara & Pablo

The project was based on the wedding of Tamara and Pablo. The bridal couple left us work freely, where we could customize the number of pieces to fit the chosen theme: the beauty of the countryside and green spaces.

Apart from the traditional invitation, we have created a series of pieces that were essential for the occasion, and were given as a souvenir for this event. We have created the main and traditional card, an indicative map of the premises where the event was held, a reminder card to save the date and an envelope. All tied with a sisal thread, according to the theme.

This project was natural, unique and bohemian like their love, which flourished in an unexpected meeting where their lives intersected. Without losing the delicateness, we used a combination of rustic aesthetic with the ornaments of old billboards to reach a vintage reminiscence. The unsaturated tones used for the flowers of the envelope, and for the lace, were intended to produce an elegant sensation. The materiality of the cards and the envelope resembled textures and fibers from plants.

Ana & Sergio

Design Agency: Regio   Client: Ana & Sergio

Ana and Sergio were graphic designers in Bogota who decided to embark on the adventure of marriage. Lovers of typography, analog design and bluegrass folk music, this alternative couple wanted cards that covered their names in a lettering and diverse typographical compositions with all information necessary for this romantic event. They also wanted additional detail that could surprise the guests.

After inquiring for their graphic and musical interests of the partner, we designed cards in an unconventional format: a poster with a phrase that identified the faith of this young couple "Two are more than one". We chose a graphic style inspired by the southern country music posters and we designed lettering with decorative letters, very similar to the announcements made for Bluegrass discs.

In wedding cards every detail concerning the information was very important, so we decided to clarify the information sections that gave indications so that all guests could understand, such as suggestions apparel, gift lists, phone numbers to confirm attendance and most relevant: date (taking a complete module). In the end, we made a tour map so that all attendees could come without problems.

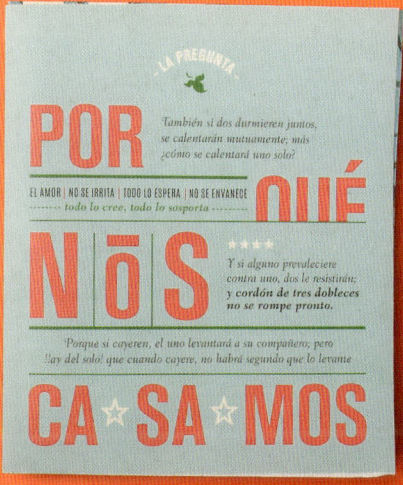

A Wedding Invitation

Designer: Dũng Trần

This was an invitation card for my old friend's wedding. It was such an interesting project, we talked a lot about the wedding plan, the decoration, the great songs would be played, the beautiful day was going to be, the charming bride and groom, the poem would be read by a cute friend on that day, so that I had great inspirations to create this small invitation card for their wedding.

To my dear friends, I hope your life together will be filled with joy, happiness and lots of love!

"Doubt that the stars are like fire;

Doubt that the sun doesn't move;

Doubt truth to be a liar;

But never doubt your love;

Best wishes for the future!"

N & M Wedding Cards

Designer: María Sanz Ricarte   Client: Noelia & Manuel   Photographer: El Calotipo

Designing wedding invitations is always a beautiful and special process, and when the couple wants to represent a point in time of their love story, it is even more exceptional.

Noelia and Manuel, were a charming couple who met in Portuguese classes. When I was asked to design their wedding invitations, this love for Portuguese culture that had brought them together, was the main idea they wanted me to portray. I designed a cheerful, simple and colorful invitation upon this theme, playing with different fonts and patterns inspired by famous Portuguese tiles that brought plenty of vitality.

Designed in an original vertical format and in two inks, these invitations were made with the letterpress printing technique, on a high quality cottonpaper, which gave them such a special texture.

In addition, a drawing of a map as original as useful was included in a way that some guests could get lost.

Ola & Daniel Wedding Invitation

Graphic Design + Art Direction: Nina Gregier   Photography: Nina Gregier

This wedding invitation for Ola & Daniel was printed on an eco paper in a natural color, laminated with two sheets. To get white graphics and texts on such a thick paper I used the silkscreen printing technique, which gave a nice structure on the smooth paper. Additional element was a black stamp with the logo of Ola & Daniel wedding party placed on the envelope.

The style of graphic design refers to the romantic / bohemian location and interior design of an old, renovated granary building, where the wedding party took place.

Wedding Invitation

Designer: Kei and Jet Tawara

This modern and art deco design was crafted by the designers for their own wedding. It was inspired by the vintage signage and postcards. Hand-drawn elements perfectly intertwined with geometric shapes. A minimal palette was chosen for simplicity and to give the invitation a classic look.

The names were framed within a large stylized version of a diamond ring. An outline of the Eiffel Tower alluded to the location of the event. To simplify the RSVP process, a website link was used with a secret password. The card was complete when paired with an envelope lined with a corresponding pattern.

Wedding Invites

Designer: Jonathan Lawrence/ Amelia Lawrence
Client: Jonathan & Amelia Lawrence   Printing: Alee & Press
Stamps: Southern Stamp Company   Photography: Amelia Lawrence

Invitation suite for our destination wedding at Washington Oaks State Park, in Palm Coast, Florida (USA).